Unbroken

Aidan O'Mahony is a Kerry Gaelic football player who has won five All-Irelands, three NFL titles and ten Munster Championships. In the 2006 All-Ireland Final against Mayo, Aidan was selected as RTÉ Man of the Match and he also won All-Star Awards in 2006 and 2007. He announced his retirement from inter-county football in 2017, having made 70 championship appearances and featured in 85 league games for Kerry. In March 2017, he won the first ever *Dancing with the Stars Ireland* with his dance partner Valeria Milova. Aidan is a passionate member of An Garda Síochána. In 2018, Aidan tapped into his core interest and love of training and fitness and set up AOM Fitness. He is married to Denise Healy and has two little girls, Lucia and Lilah.

AIDAN O'MAHONY
UNBROKEN

A JOURNEY OF ADVERSITY, MENTAL
STRENGTH AND PHYSICAL FITNESS

HACHETTE
BOOKS
IRELAND

First published in Ireland in 2021 by

HACHETTE BOOKS IRELAND

1

Written with Michael Moynihan

Cataloguing in Publication Data is available from the British Library

ISBN 9781529344363

Typeset in Sabon by The Little Red Pen Publishing Services

Printed and bound in Great Britain by
Clays Ltd, Elcograf, S.p.A

Hachette Books Ireland policy is to use papers that are natural, renewable and recyclable products and made from wood grown in sustainable forests. The logging and manufacturing processes are expected to conform to the environmental regulations of the country of origin.

Hachette Books Ireland
8 Castlecourt Centre
Castleknock
Dublin 15, Ireland
A division of Hachette UK Ltd
Carmelite House, 50 Victoria Embankment, EC4Y 0DZ
www.hachettebooksireland.ie

Contents

With thanks to Michael Moynihan for his help in writing this book.

And also thanks to Michael O'Donoghue.

Introduction

Everyone's rock bottom is different.

For me, that time came in early 2010. I'd given up inter-county football. I was going to work and coming home from work, going to club training and coming home from training: a continuous routine without enjoyment. I wasn't happy; a constant feeling of being down and not finding happiness in anything can be a heavy burden.

I felt alone and my mind was on severe overdrive. I couldn't get any peace and I wasn't myself. That was clear to me.

I was at home the morning I began the journey to change that. While I wouldn't have seen my parents cry too often, my father in particular, they cried that morning. That was difficult for them, and difficult for me. They were seeing their son, almost 30 years of age, in a broken state and wondering how things had reached that stage.

I was losing the person I'd grown up to be: all my family wanted was what was best for me.

I got into the car outside my home with my eldest sister, Nora, someone who's always been there for me and was very close to me, and we set off.

It was probably a tough journey for her. There wasn't much conversation. I spent the drive looking out the window as the miles reeled by.

Looking back now, I'd always felt I was a person who didn't need help – I didn't need counselling, coaching, support or advice from anyone. That conformed to the surface impression people had of me: teak-tough on the pitch, someone up for the physical and mental challenge of sport.

But off the field?

Things had been building up inside me for years, dating all the way back to the time I was diagnosed with asthma as a very young child. I didn't discuss that at any point in life, or how I felt about it, and that was the template I followed ever afterwards; that was also the template that led to that trip in the car.

It was a dark day and the sky was filled with greyness, which suited the mood. I felt as though I had a physical weight on me. I wasn't worried about what lay ahead of me on that journey: I was questioning myself, whether

I'd made the right decision and whether my destination was what I really needed to exit the dark place I was in.

Nora was attempting to make conversation with me, but I barely opened my mouth. She was probably hoping that the experience ahead of me would change my outlook given how negative I was at that time, feeling there was nothing good in my life.

I couldn't see the positive in work, family or football, and I was the one who'd allowed things get to that state. People are more forthcoming now about their challenges, and how they speak about those challenges, but I wasn't. I was a closed book.

That's not a loose description. I wasn't an open person and didn't discuss my feelings.

We pulled up to the big black gates of our destination and once we passed through I saw the gardens – the flowers and manicured lawns – and immediately it was therapeutic. There was some solace in the surroundings, in feeling I'd done the right thing in taking that initial step.

I walked through the doors of the Aiséirí centre. Aiséirí is known as a centre for the treatment of addictions but they also take people without addiction issues who just need counselling and some time out, and as soon as I entered the building I knew I'd made the right decision.

My attitude then was that I needed to step away from the real world. I didn't feel one-to-one counselling would be enough, a scenario where you have a counselling session and then back to work or off to training.

If I had been more open all along maybe I wouldn't have had to go into Aiséirí, but the other side of that is that the experience there changed my life. I found myself again during my six weeks in there and I will never forget that feeling.

There's no contact with the outside world – one of the reasons I chose to go there in the first place – no phones, no social media. It's just about you and getting yourself right.

When I walked through the doors that day I felt a release, and while there I reflected on my challenges and found solutions to my problems. People often refer to the road less travelled, and taking that road changed my life.

I'm more open than I was because of those six weeks. Lockdown throughout the pandemic has taught us all what's important – that human contact with family and friends is crucial for all of us. Talking is therapy!

I learned that lesson in Aiséirí and I've never forgotten it. There's no sport in the centre, but there was a big field at the back of the facility. That space was a huge outlet for me.

I'd go for a run/sprint up and down the hills three times a day. Do my 100-plus press-ups and 100-plus sit-ups at six o'clock in the morning when I got up, the same at night before going to bed.

As soon as my head hit the pillow then at 10 p.m. I switched off and slept deeply. Removing myself from the sports world was an important part of the process: in the preceding couple of years I'd had the controversy of both the Donncha O'Connor incident and the positive drugs test (relating to inhaler use for my asthma), and removing myself from those dramatic events helped me as well.

What the process helped me to do specifically was to find the young person I was and the pathway that gave me peace. I was able to tease out what it was I enjoyed in life and to rediscover that.

On the last day there's a ceremony where you burn papers which have your negative thoughts. After that I walked out the gate to be collected by my other sister, Linda. I was a different person. My shoulders were back, my chest out: I'd found myself and was proud of what I'd done.

It's not the answer for everyone. If everyone's rock bottom is different then everyone's way out of that can be different as well. I don't claim to be an expert on mental health: I can only speak about what's helped me. I was on the floor and the experience was a huge help to me.

I'm a more positive, caring person because of that. Travelling home in the car with Linda that day we had a full conversation about how everyone was getting on: it wasn't a superficial chat, but real, honest communication. My sister Linda is an expert communicator and has established a very successful business based on this skill. She has an extremely positive outlook and I learn a lot from her approach to life. My two sisters always offered me support and guidance during this time.

My parents were thrilled to see me when we arrived home that day; they recognised the change in me immediately.

The benefits weren't limited to my social skills. Shortly after I was back playing football, I fell in with my club, Rathmore, for a game against Laune Rangers and I had a top performance.

Flying, but not infallible! After that game there was a photograph in the newspaper of me having been planted on my backside by one of the Rangers players. The caption? 'Fallen Idol'.

I asked myself whether that was how I wanted to be remembered, but there was a difference in my motivation. I was more driven than I'd ever been but now the drive was unbelievably positive, not negative.

1

Inspiration All Around Me

Growing Up in Rathmore

I'm from Mounthorgan, just under the Pap mountains, on the Killarney side of Rathmore. The terrain around the house is rugged: our back garden is made up of glens and mountains. Our farm is in Glenflesk, a neighbouring parish, and sits in the middle of the mountains, with a long narrow winding road leading up to some of the most breathtaking views in the county – and to some of the hardest and longest climbs you take as a farmer.

Stepping out our back door, straight across the yard is a stone house that's now a cowshed. It used to be a home – home to a family of eight. These days it shelters four cattle but serves as a reminder of what my father grew up in.

That wasn't on my radar when I was young, an appreciation for that, but looking back now I can see where a lot of my traits came from. Around our house that reminder of hard work never left: there was a constant buzz of activity, a tractor travelling the road and machinery buzzing. Mounthorgan is a strong farming area.

My mom is still with us but sadly my dad passed away in 2012. My mom was a housewife and my dad worked in the Cadbury's chocolate factory in Rathmore, while we had a farm as well – sheep and cattle.

Dad was a Rathmore native and Mom is from Glenflesk. She went to America for a number of years but came back to marry my dad, so I grew up in Rathmore rather than Long Island. I have a lot of family still out in Long Island, as my aunts went to America with my mom.

My father, Thade, was a factory worker who tended his land, cattle and sheep in all hours outside of his 'normal' work shift – sitting idle wasn't the norm in our house and even my relatives, those coming to us for a holiday, were given jobs. This graft has transitioned to all my siblings, as they are all grafters in different professions, from law to entrepreneurship, to IT and engineering. My four brothers and two sisters are all inspirational to me; being the youngest, their leadership was always something I admired.

We credit the habit of not sitting still to our father, who was constantly on the move, always keeping busy. Coming in the door from a shift in the factory, he'd head straight back out again. That was the norm – nothing said, just went about his work.

That attitude is actually common throughout our local area, like on the summer days in the bog when you could never get enough help – any help you got was welcome – and then the sense of relief seeing your neighbours coming to give a hand was like no other.

Although it soon wore off once you realised you'd have to return the favour down the line.

A lot of the clichés about kids growing up in rural Ireland weren't clichés for us: they were true. There were just four kids in my class in Shrone national school and only two classrooms in the school – one for a teacher and the other for the principal, Dan Vincent O'Connor, who lived up the road. He played a huge part in my development and in fostering a love for Gaelic football. It was a very small community and a very small school.

Our summers consisted of cutting hay or getting on the bike and heading out to explore the hills that surrounded Rathmore – outdoor adventures with neighbours were really the height of entertainment. I might leave the house at 9 a.m. and come back at 11 p.m. when it got dark – meeting up with your pals, going to different houses, but mostly just cycling around the area or climbing the endless trees.

One of the big highlights for me growing up was getting a licence to drive the tractor in my teens. That meant I could go up and down the road where I lived, embrace a little freedom, and go off and cut hay to make a contribution to the household.

There wasn't a nightlife scene for teens in Rathmore. The nearest disco was the Hiland in Newmarket – a real disco, as in a venue for adults – but that wasn't even a distant spot on the horizon for me as a kid.

For the first 15 or 16 years of my life farming was what I did and farming was what I wanted to do.

It's a particular type of farming in our part of the world. You have grassland in the area, but then you also have hills and mountains divided up between different people – miles upon miles of terrain to cover.

Our particular mountain backed onto the Pap mountains, and there's a drop between the two, and I would spend weekends with my brothers walking over hills and mountains for miles from morning to night, checking up on our sheep to make sure they were safe.

Anyone who has sheep will know the feeling – you're out for hours and you find 10 of them, but there's still one missing. So back out you go to find it; you'd never leave one of them behind. The steps were definitely through the roof back then: I didn't need a Garmin or Apple Watch to tell me when I'd done over 10,000 for the day.

The trail to find sheep meant walking for hours over hills and mountains, climbing steep edges and endless rocks, the kind of exercise that would definitely stand to me later in my sporting career.

At one stage I remember we got a gift of binoculars sent from relatives in America, and it was like having a GPS device parachuted in from the future. You could pick out the JH brand in blue painted on the side of the sheep wool. Every farmer has a different brand or colour to distinguish their flock, so it was easier to pick them out in the distance – but you had to go after them if they'd strayed away too far.

The work was still very physical all round. If you wanted to feed sheep, then all of the hay and nuts would have to be brought up through the fields across your shoulders, as no tractors could travel up the mountains. No shortcuts.

It was a fair test of my strength, but it was also the ideal weight programme for a young boy. I can honestly say that I loved the whole experience, especially the turn of the seasons.

In the summer I used to go to the bog. Anyone from the country will know the work involved: all the neighbours' kids would come along and everyone pitched in to create a real sense of community.

I know there are those who might think that such physical work wasn't suitable for children, but we genuinely didn't feel like that. We grew up with it and enjoyed it, and in terms of fitness for sport it certainly helped me later on as I knew what it felt like to work physically hard.

I'm not sure how many kids nowadays would do that, which isn't a criticism. Children are protected a lot more now and are not subjected to strenuous or physical work. If a child has football training or dancing or some other commitment, they're driven there and picked up, while we were encouraged to cycle for miles for any extra-curricular activities.

Times have changed very quickly: my childhood was far less complex than the average child's experience nowadays. We had milk from our own cows, meat from our own sheep and cows, fruit and vegetables from our garden. Very simple.

Growing up, I always thought I'd be a farmer. I can even remember buying my first sheep at 15 or 16 and thinking there'd be plenty more.

Education was very important to my parents, something that my siblings and I are very thankful for now. We would never have been allowed to miss school. I grew up in an academic house where we were encouraged to do homework and work to the best of our ability.

At the weekends and during school holidays I used to go to fairs with my eldest brother, Noel. We'd come home at nightfall with new sheep, and we'd put our brand on them – the JH – and the neighbours would come in to see what we'd bought. And of course the following day the sheep would have scattered all over the place and you'd spend days looking for them around the mountains.

During the summers we'd also dip sheep – immersing them in a concrete tank full of water and insecticide to kill off any parasites – and again, that was very exciting for a kid like me, because there was a huge commotion and bustle about it. After school I used to get the homework done as quickly as possible so I could head off out to the farm in Glenflesk.

Farming's a hard life, and you get used to the rhythm of it. In the winter you're out in terrible weather, cold and wet, looking for sheep.

You have to bring in the cows for the winter, usually November, depending on the weather, which is another big job, trying to tie cows to a wall in a shed, and every day you've to feed them.

The sheep are different. They're out on the grass until October or November, then they're put up on the mountain, and you don't have much more to do with them until January or February – though you've to bring them nuts and hay daily, and if there was a bad winter you might bring them down to the fields during January.

Then there's lambing season in March, which is a big part of the year. Every evening around that time that's all I wanted to do, to go back up around Glenflesk to see if there were new lambs there.

This young farmer here wasn't always that professional either. Come time for the fair, there might be 100 lambs down by the house and I'd try to hide some of them so they wouldn't be taken away to the fair.

My dad and Noel would go through them and assess them all. 'That's a fine ewe,' they might say. 'It'll survive on the mountain so we'll keep on to it.'

And I'd say, 'We'll keep on to this one too.'

But they'd disagree, and those ones would go into the trailer.

Growing up, I probably spent most of my childhood with Noel. Following his lead, always trying to impress him with my farming ability.

The area was small, safe and remote. As a kid you were protected – but the other side of that was your social skills might not have been at the same level as someone who was in a big school in a town.

Again, that's not a complaint. Looking back, it was a good childhood, great to keep you grounded, but I was very much an introverted kid. Our area was built on teamwork: summers were fine, winters were tough, but you could always be sure that a neighbour was there to offer that helping hand. In our small townland of Shrone we have a church overlooking the valley; built and funded by the community, it highlights the importance of solidarity.

The only downside was that very remoteness from the outside world. Looking back, between the sheer physical isolation, and being in a primary school class of four kids, your skills in social situations wouldn't be the most sophisticated. As a result, I definitely felt my personality development suffered.

I wouldn't be someone to come into a roomful of strangers and be the loudest in the room. That's part shyness and part my upbringing, which was a very happy one, without necessarily involving a lot of socialising.

I loved being on the farm, but away from the farm I was quiet. Going to secondary school was a big change. It is for anyone, but I was coming from a class of four children I'd known my entire life to a school with hundreds of kids.

The only major shadow over my childhood was severe asthma. As far back as I can remember, even though I was physically strong, I'd always notice a tightness in my chest on the cold mornings – I still do – and in the summer when turning hay. I knew that something was not right; I'd regularly find myself short of breath but thought it was part of the hard work so I'd battle through, eventually having to take a rest.

Still, the days outdoors pushing the lungs to their limit would catch up with me at night time.

Once my head hit the pillow the uncontrollable coughing and wheezing would start, ending up with me struggling for breath and eventually being put into the backseat of Mom and Dad's car heading for the local doctor.

When people ask me about asthma now I tell them it's like putting a bag over your head, trying to breathe, and that shortness of breath – and then trying to carry on with life as well.

I was eventually diagnosed with asthma when I was eight, because I was constantly having breathing problems up to that age. In bed at night, I'd be trying to catch my breath … thinking about it now, the memory is vivid, that shortness of breath, gasping for air.

Back then we didn't have the same facilities that are available now to kids who are asthmatic. Nowadays you can talk to someone about living with asthma; back then you just got on with it, really.

I felt like a burden at home, more than anything else, because of it. I missed a lot of school as a result of my sickness, and the local GP was probably up in our house more than any other house in the parish.

I can remember all the details: going into his house and getting up on a green bed there to take the nebuliser. That freed up my breathing temporarily and I could relax again for a little while.

If I close my eyes I can hear the nebuliser, the sound of it whirring. I had to get a number of injections growing up and I've a fear of needles ever since – I still hate them to this day, no matter how small. After the treatment the doctor would say, 'How do you feel now?' But after another look at me he might decide, 'No, we'll have to hospitalise him.' You look back and you think, *What a massive pain in the butt it must have been for my parents.*

When I say I felt like a burden, it's with good reason: my parents would regularly also have to drive me to hospital in Tralee, an hour away, and most of those trips were late at night.

I was very conscious of it, of being the one in the house who was sick a lot of the time – any time I got a cold it would trigger the asthma. I'd be the only one who'd be missing school regularly, the only one who had to be minded if I wanted to go out and about. I used to keep my family awake so many nights due to the asthma.

When I did play football, particularly as a small kid, the asthma held me back. I'd only get 10 or 15 minutes on the field from the coaches, as they knew I wouldn't last any longer. Because of that I didn't have the interest in football or sport and I wasn't developing as a player.

This should not intimidate kids who have asthma now. Treatments have advanced greatly since I was a child, while the support systems around the condition, from online forums to personal counselling, are so much better.

Back then it was a Ventolin inhaler which you used if you felt an attack coming on. If that happened morning, noon or night, then so be it; a preventative measure, pure and simple.

Eventually the asthma became a barrier that I couldn't cross. If I was running as part of training in school, for instance, I'd give in to it every time – as soon as I started to struggle. The irony is that nowadays if I'm talking to kids with asthma I tell them not to let the asthma define them mentally; back then it certainly defined me.

I didn't want it to, absolutely not. I didn't want to be getting out of bed at three in the morning to tell my parents I couldn't breathe, with the result that the doctor had to come to the house or we had to set out in the car for the hospital in Tralee.

While it was great to be out and about all summer, I was also out and about with hay everywhere, which led to hay fever – and this triggered my asthma.

In winter, particularly playing sport, my breathing was always affected. Nowadays you'd often hear coaches and managers telling players to get their second wind: an asthmatic might need a third or fourth wind to kick in before they're comfortable.

At underage level in particular it's a lot easier not to get involved rather than challenge your lungs to work that hard. There were plenty of examples: I remember one time in secondary school we had a run to do as part of PE – it was 5K and I remember thinking, *I'm not going to finish this.*

The real irony is that it took me so long to recognise that exercise actually helped me deal with it. The more I exercised, the better I felt. I don't presume to speak for anyone else's condition, but I know myself that the more exercise I got, the less severe my asthma got, and exercise became more of a benefit to me than a trigger for asthma.

Because of the asthma, sport wasn't a burning obsession for me as a young kid. I played a bit of badminton with my brother Anthony, and he was also involved in Old Chapel Rovers soccer team so I started playing with them at a young age, under his guidance. This was my first experience of watching an athlete so driven and determined no matter what sport he played. You could see he was the ultimate competitor, a team player, and more importantly he was respected by all his team-mates.

I was playing Gaelic football with Rathmore as well, and by the time I got to 16 or so I began to take notice of other players around my own age. Players I knew at school who weren't just playing minor but under-21, maybe, and I started thinking, *Why am I not playing at that level? Why am I not playing minor at 16?*

I could reason my way through to the answer: I felt I had the footballing talent but I was nervous about pushing myself because of the asthma, and I felt the asthma meant coaches and managers didn't trust me to last longer than 20 minutes in a game.

But coming into March, April, the days were getting brighter and longer, and the asthma was improving. It's amazing how the mind works – in January, February, the start of March I'd be thinking, *I'm not able for training in this*, because of the cold and frost, but once April hit and the temperatures picked up, things started to improve.

It became a trigger point for me, finishing those laps while training with Rathmore. I started to view it as though the asthma was there but it was a barrier to push past – and once I got past it, it was gone.

Instead of thinking in a match, *I've made five runs now, there's no way I'll manage another one because the asthma will come on*, I was beginning to realise that the asthma wasn't being triggered. I started to train myself mentally to deal with it.

That became a template for me as life went on, an early lesson in resilience. To see an obstacle or a problem – on the playing field or off – and to recognise it for what it was, to break it down, to look into myself for a solution or a strategy to get past it or resolve it.

Learning to do that with asthma and football in particular was crucial, because it tied a lot of different strands together for me: confidence and football, competitiveness and self-reliance. It was a road map for what was to come.

I came to accept that I didn't choose asthma – it chose me, I told myself, and I have to live with that. My brother John, who is also asthmatic, would have given me plenty of tips and reassurance on living with asthma and not letting it define me. I took his advice, and throughout my career John would play a massive part in my sporting achievements, from those little phone calls to putting a roof over my head as I started my garda career in

Limerick, something for which I'm forever grateful to John and his wife Thrish.

Eventually, though, I got the breakthrough that started my sporting career. I got a phone call one morning that Rathmore senior football team were short and needed a corner-back. I was due to play a soccer game but fell in with Rathmore instead.

There seems to be a trend nowadays for people to look externally for motivation or inspiration – whether it's that 'guest speaker' for a function or just scrolling through social media for quotes or short videos.

A lesson I learned is that you don't have to look that far from your own surroundings for motivation or inspiration.

The small accomplishments are every bit as important as the big ones. Hard work was shown to me from day one – I could list a thousand examples, but take my father, who would work a farm around a factory shift during the day and still be the first one into the car to bring me to a game.

Consistency, hard work, no excuses, there are no special quotes needed: just look around you, take notice and use your own story to fuel yourself.

2

Confronting My Doubts

Making Strides with the Minors

Playing for the Kerry minors hadn't really been a target for me. It might have been something that occurred to other promising players in the county, lads who'd be thinking, *I'm going well here at under-15, under-16, I'm in with a shout*. But not for me.

I was knocking more fun out of the soccer at the time. I loved playing with my brother Anthony every weekend, there was no pressure and I was playing well as a centre-half who didn't believe in messing around on the ball. Mick McCarthy would have warmed to my style of play, I'd say. But coming to 1998, I was just turning 18. Seamus Cooper took over the Rathmore senior team, and one morning I ended up filling a gap for the footballers at corner-back.

Straightaway it was different to playing soccer. I noticed that immediately. It's more embedded in the community. There was a bigger crowd at the game to keep an eye on what was going on. People were taking it more seriously. For all that, the job of a corner-back was very straightforward. Mark your man, pure and simple. If he isn't seen and you aren't seen, it's a win for you as a defender.

I did okay that day, and a few weeks into that season we went on a long trip to Gallarus on the Dingle peninsula to take on An Gaeltacht. They had a massive team (Ó Cinnéide, Mac Gearailt, all the Ó Sés), and the pitch itself in Gallarus was almost as big a challenge. You'd nearly want to go over the weather forecast in detail to know what to expect when you landed there, to get an idea of which way the wind might be blowing – and the Gaeltacht lads knew to a T how to play that wind.

It's a full day's travel from Rathmore out to Gallarus. We stopped at a pub outside Dingle for sandwiches and a cup of tea on the way before getting all the way out to the edge of the Atlantic for the game. I ended up marking Dara Ó Cinnéide for a spell that day and I did alright.

He kicked two or three points, but that was reasonable enough, and I was happy in how I did – he was a top, top forward at the time, after all.

On the way back we broke the journey as well. Lads had a couple of pints and a bite to eat, and I can remember, despite having lost the game, the sense of enjoyment, the feeling of fulfilment and accomplishment – whatever you want to call it. Looking back, it was a matter of the entire community – or near enough to it – packing up en masse and heading back to west Kerry.

The way everyone fell in together and stopped in the one place for sandwiches and a drink on the way home … these were people who'd coached and nurtured me as a kid, and here they were again supporting me and the others in the club's senior team.

It really left an impression on me – that people would give up their time and effort when you were a kid and then would drop everything to give over a whole Sunday to following the team. It's a really organic connection, and the other reason it left that impression on me was that I hadn't been that interested in Gaelic games as a small kid, so when I saw that link, the bond between the community and the club, up close it made an even bigger mark on me.

It's a day out, and it's enjoyable for people, but it's still a powerful bond that builds between everyone.

At the time I'd finished school and had a summer job plastering – hard work, which I never minded. Up and into a van at 6 a.m. to travel to Cork, back by teatime, but I had a few quid in my pocket and the lads were good company. All was right with the world.

When we went back training after the Gaeltacht game, on the Tuesday evening, Seamus Cooper said to me, 'Look, I've been onto Charlie Nelligan [the Kerry minor manager] and I told him you should be inside with the Kerry minors.' This was an extraordinary leap of faith as I was never a standout player underage, never mind standing out for the Rathmore team, but he saw something in me that I couldn't see myself. Charlie agreed to Seamus's request and I went in for a few trial games with the Kerry minors and it's interesting now to look back at the attitude I brought into those games.

Derry Crowley – father of Johnny, who I would later play with in the Kerry senior team – would pick us up in The Reeks petrol station in Killarney and I'd start looking around at the lads in the car, and thinking about the others waiting at training. I'd pick a first 15 out of all of them, then pick the five or six subs, and try to work out if I could slip myself in among the subs: was I worth a place there?

That was my attitude. I didn't back myself. To be fair, though, there was a lot of quality in that particular Kerry team. I didn't know a lot of the players personally but there's a bush telegraph in every county. Everyone knows well who the stars in their age groups are.

For instance, on that minor team there were three Ronan O'Connors – from Kilcummin, Ballyduff and Foilmore – Stephen O'Sullivan was in his second year playing minor and was a senior two years after that, Marc Ó Sé was in from the Gaeltacht, Tadhg Kennelly, Seán O'Sullivan, Eoin Brosnan, Kevin Lynch ...

It was a very good crop, and that time I used to read *The Kingdom* newspaper every week – looking out for my own name in the match reports, obviously, but these guys' names were popping up everywhere. They were the future of Kerry football, earmarked for bigger things already. Playing under-21 for Kerry. Playing senior.

We would head in to minor training, do our 10 or 15 laps of the pitch, then fall in for a game. I'd be on the B team, full- or centre-back.

The standard was very good. I could end up marking a savage athlete like Tadhg Kennelly, someone I might be able to hold for 40 minutes of the game ... and then bang! He'd hit me for 1–2 in five minutes.

Or else it was Seán O'Sullivan or Eoin Brosnan, two lads with unbelievable engines, who'd run all day – and run direct and hard, more to the point.

There was no gym culture for underage players back then, so I wouldn't have been considered a big hitter by any means, but it began to dawn on me gradually that my day job was benefiting me. That was rewarding in itself. Spending weeks working with plasterers was having an effect.

If you spent eight hours a day drawing five-gallon drums of sand and cement up four flights of stairs, Monday to Friday, it was bound to make you stronger.

I learned from the sessions as well. One evening in with Kerry, someone brought up the elements of tackling and gobbling up the player in possession, so I started to put all of those pieces together – the strength I was building with the manual work alongside the technique I was picking up. I was improving as the sessions wore on. I could see that in my physique and in my tackling.

The running, though, was something to survive, a period of the session where I just about hung in there and got through.

It wasn't a physical test so much as a mental challenge. Charlie Nelligan and the other selectors were trying to work out if they could depend on lads in the last 10 minutes of an All-Ireland final or semi-final, when the chips were down, so they were putting you under that physical pressure. Could you cope with that and still be able to produce the goods?

And some of us felt that more than others. Brosnan, Kennelly, Ó Sé – they were phenomenal athletes on those runs. Going home you'd know exactly what they were wearing, down to the patterns on the soles of their boots or their runners, because they were ahead of you all evening.

For me it was all about breaking that initial barrier, because I hadn't been used to that extreme level of training that you experience at inter-county level.

When I began to play sport, at seven or eight years of age, as soon as the asthma was triggered by running, I'd stop. That's what I was taught: stop, don't push it.

But you get to inter-county level and you're exposed to something you haven't met before. And yet when the going gets tough and the breathing gets harder, your first thought is still the same – just stop.

Asthma never leaves you. It's something you have to learn to live with, and learn how to control. In my case, cold weather is the biggest trigger, or dust in the summer time. But I know now that if I'm training in cold weather, my asthma's going to be worse, and I talk to coaches and trainers about that.

And we know a lot more about it now. Back then in the minors, there wasn't the same awareness, and it was just a matter of getting through it. But now that's all changed completely.

It was a great lesson for me. Going into the dressing room first, I doubted myself. I'd be quite open about that. I doubted myself from day one instead of saying to myself, *Hang on a second – with Rathmore you're marking lads who play senior inter-county football, and the manager obviously trusts you to do that job, so what is there to be afraid of with lads your own age?*

And Rathmore were a driven club that time as well. We were trying to win a junior championship for the first time in 29 years, so I knew the standard was good there. Like every club, you know of the characters before you train with them, players who would give you the tools to mould you into the player you would become – the

O'Keeffes, the Dohertys, the Murphys, the O O'Sullivans.

I didn't think of it in those terms, though, playing alongside great players with the club, the likes of Declan O'Keeffe, Tom O'Sullivan, Gerry Murphy, Michael D. Cahill. These guys were heroes in the club, playing in a hard grade, and I was learning from them all the time.

I started to bring the quality of training with those lads into my Kerry minor training. I began to believe in myself, and the club training was strengthening that belief. I might have Kerry minor training on Sunday, Rathmore training on Tuesday and Thursday, Kerry training on Friday. I committed to all and never missed a session. There was no talk of training load that time, as you might guess from that timetable – it was a case of the more sessions, the merrier.

But it all combined to change my mindset, and that's what would help me get the better of the asthma. I wasn't the type to go to Charlie Nelligan and say, 'Look, I can't train tonight, my asthma was bad all day' – I just went and trained and got through it, and as the weather improved, the asthma became less of an issue, and I was getting fitter and stronger and more confident.

By the time the first Munster championship game came into view, against Limerick, I knew I was in with a chance of making the panel anyway. I was still doing my thing of picking the first 15 and I didn't see myself starting the match, but at that stage I could see that a spot on the bench was a real possibility.

We had a final trial game in Austin Stack Park in Tralee to settle on the panel for the Limerick match, and I was centre-back on one team.

Austin Stack Park! For me this was like the Colosseum. It was where generations of Kerry footballers had played and trained, and having this game in the stadium made it all the more real: there was a Kerry jersey close enough to be won.

They were a lot closer than I expected, in fact. Going into the dressing room that night there were jerseys given out for the trial game, the old Kerry senior jerseys. The green and gold jerseys were for one side, the blue jerseys for the other, and I remember thinking about the number 6 that I got: *Did Tim Kennelly wear this one time?*

The teams were called out, went out and warmed up, and then got straight into the game. I did something that evening that always stood to me after, though it was easier to do that night as we all warmed up together.

I watched the man I'd be marking, to see what leg he kicked from, how he hand-passed the ball, how he soloed, all of that, to get an idea of what to expect when the game itself began. My predictive skills on the pitch always benefited me.

I started well, winning the first two or three balls and getting possession. There was no great tactical approach involved, no great linking the play or dropping off as a sweeper – mark your man, one-on-one. Traditional stuff.

Everything seemed to be coming together for me. The club was going well and I felt an onus on me to back up Seamus's judgement – he was the one ringing Charlie Nelligan to bring me in and here I was, near enough to the panel.

I was feeling strong, feeling fit, winning ball in the last trial game for a place on the Kerry team. Playing Munster or All-Ireland finals was nowhere near the radar, but the prospect of a Kerry jersey – the number didn't matter – was close enough to drive me on.

About 15 minutes into the game I got in a block down, but the ball bounced straight back up again. I reached my hand across to get it and got an unmerciful bang into the face. Down I went.

My eyes were closed, and I remember thinking, *This isn't good anyway*, but I was able to get up.

I looked down and saw that the front of my jersey was covered in blood. One or two players came over but turned away saying, 'Jesus Christ', which wasn't encouraging.

Charlie and Derry came over to have a look and one of them said, 'It's not too bad, I'd say,' which wasn't that encouraging either.

At that stage I didn't know where I got the hit, whether it was my eye or my nose or my jaw – looking back, I was definitely concussed – but none of the commentary I was hearing made me feel any better. I was brought into the dressing room and Derry sent me in to wash myself in the shower.

I came out and he examined my face – I still didn't know what had happened – and eventually I found a mirror in the dressing room. I saw my nose had gone over to my ear, almost, with a fine mark across the top where a stud had caught me.

'It's not that bad,' Derry kept telling me.

'Derry, what are you looking at?' was my response.

The blood wouldn't stop pouring out but Derry drove me down to the hospital, where eventually they stopped the bleeding by inserting cotton and matchsticks.

The doctor told me to come back two weeks later to have it reset.

Rathmore were training two nights later but I wasn't allowed to take part – I had a severe fracture of the nose, the bridge was damaged, there was internal bleeding, all of that.

I wasn't disappointed, though, and I was ready to come back soon enough, but the county board told me I'd have to be written off for a month from playing football or I wouldn't be covered by insurance. And as eager as I was to get back, I missed the Munster semi-final and final.

It was tough. I didn't go to the games, either. At that time if you were out injured you wouldn't be brought along as part of the group, but I wasn't a great man to go to watch Kerry games anyway. (It might surprise people, but the first Kerry senior game I ever saw in the flesh was the 1996 All-Ireland semi-final against Mayo.)

I fell back in with the club, though, and trained very hard – and loved it. It was as though the shackles were taken off. I was back with the lads I knew and everything was coming together. The asthma was under control, the fitness was built up, the characters in the club were great – we had the likes of Donie O'Connor and Tim Cronin in midfield, whose approach in training toughened you up no matter what age you were, put it that way.

Donal Dineen, Dermie Fitz and Padraig Murphy would give you a run for your money every night you had to mark them at training – I was learning the meaning of the club from all these guys.

It was a virtuous circle. Tough training with Rathmore got me right to train with the Kerry minors, and tough training with Kerry had me well primed when I fell back in with Rathmore, and I kept those standards up.

As a result, I was called back into the Kerry minor panel after the Munster final in July. Kerry were in an All-Ireland semi-final and I remember thinking there was a chance of action, and that I'd do everything I could for the few weeks' run-in to that match to make the panel.

The improvement was visible when I went back in with the minors. I could see it myself. In the running I was closer to the man ahead of me. At the start of the year there might be 20 yards between us, but now I was right up with the rest of them. I was enjoying it, I was believing in myself, and Charlie had a few chats with me which encouraged and motivated me as well.

After one of the last training sessions before the game, Derry dropped me to Killarney, to where my parents would pick me up at The Reeks, and as I got out of the car he gave me the word: 'You're on the panel for the All-Ireland semi-final.'

I can remember thinking, *Control yourself here*, as I got into my parents' car. They asked how I'd got on and I told them. I was on the panel for the weekend.

In all my time playing for Kerry I have two great memories of my parents, and one was that night in particular, telling them the news as I got into the car.

It was huge for me, huge for my parents – they had become more interested in football as a result of me getting more involved, but that night I could see the pure pride in them. Their posture straightened up immediately, they were so proud, and that also made me proud.

I owe a lot of my playing achievements to my parents and family, because they're the ones who put the time in with me for years. They were well entitled to get a kick out of any success or recognition that I got, and I've never forgotten the delight they got out of that news that evening.

I was chuffed with myself when I got the official Kerry gear. A tracksuit and top that I valued greatly.

The hype around it was terrific. That Thursday morning my mom went over the road to get the papers, and there it was, the name in black and white: Aidan O'Mahony (Rathmore).

I went over to training one evening that week in Rathmore to say thanks to Seamus Cooper and the lads for believing in me. Everyone in life needs someone to show that kind of faith in them, and by doing so Seamus made a huge difference to my career.

As a panellist your attitude is always going to be a bit different. Nowadays if I were talking to players I'd be pointing out to substitutes that they need to be tuned in, that they need to believe they're as good as the lads starting – because a point in the game will come when some of them have to come into the action and they'll need to get involved immediately when they do.

But back then, I took the old advice of 'taking it all in' to heart. I made sure I appreciated the whole experience, start to finish, of being involved in an All-Ireland semi-final.

I finished the manual work on the Thursday – they paid me for the Friday as well, which was a bonus – and

I spent a lot of the Friday sporting the Kerry gear: that short-sleeved top stretched almost all the way down to the knuckles.

I met up with the rest of the panel in Killarney on the Saturday and it started to sink in: I'm one of the 24 here.

That feeling continued when we got on the bus, because I was worried about where to sit and who to sit with, of course.

Now it'd be great to call to mind who I sat with, but the strongest memory of that trip was the destination, the Tara Towers hotel, because I was like a small child on his summer holidays when I got there.

On the way up, though, I remember thinking that I'd been sitting in the stands watching Kerry in the 1996 All-Ireland and now, two years later, I was going to get out onto the Croke Park pitch. The difference in two years was what filled my head, not who I was sitting next to.

I wasn't even thinking about the following day because I was so wrapped up in the bonding with those players.

That night in the hotel Charlie Nelligan came around to all of us individually for a chat, and on one level you're listening to him talk about the game the following day, and on the other you're thinking, *This guy has seven All-Ireland medals and he's chatting to me.*

For the first time in my life I started to get a few butterflies. People were talking about the jersey and what it means, and the penny started to drop. You're just

18 and enjoying the experience, but there's an awful lot riding on the following day. You're not wearing any old jersey: you're getting to wear a jersey that the greatest players ever have worn, because the vast majority of those players started off as county minors.

Despite all of that, though, I slept very well that night.

To show how things have changed, breakfast the following morning was anything you wanted. Literally.

Full fry-up, sausages, rashers and eggs? No problem. Pint of milk with that? Help yourself. No porridge or flaxseed to be seen, which is very different to the menu nowadays.

We were playing Laois, who were the benchmark that time in underage football – Beano McDonald was the big name but they had other very good players as well. But we had a very strong team also.

The tactics were straightforward: man versus man, which would obviously suit a sub's prospects, because if someone was in trouble it was because their direct opponent was getting on top of them, not some breakdown in the defensive system. In that case a direct replacement would be needed, the 'shepherd's hook' would come out and a sub would be sent in.

There was silence in the bus on the way into the stadium. Then gradually, as we moved along, the crowds on the street started getting thicker and thicker, there were more and more county jerseys to be seen, the air horns were going off, people were roaring up at the bus – this was a different world to the football I'd been playing.

There might be a couple of hundred at a big game down in Rathbeg and here I was on a bus nosing through thousands of people in Dublin, the flags on those old bamboo sticks, the old-style peaked caps in county colours.

When we got into the stadium it was quiet enough, obviously, an hour before the minor game, but my jaw still dropped when we got out onto the field – there's no other way to describe it. Croke Park was overwhelming.

I remember looking down towards the Davin end and seeing a hollow in the field, a dip, and being surprised by that (even though as a surface it was still a lot better than what I was used to).

The middle of the field was painted with the GAA crest. I was looking up at the height of the stands towering overhead.

I was tuned in and ready if I was needed, but I was still a sub, so maybe I was able to take that step back and appreciate it, to take in the privilege that I was enjoying.

There was no pressure on me, sitting on the bench, and to be honest I didn't think I'd get game time. Charlie had said to me to be ready to come on, but I was thinking, *Ah, he's saying that to every fella now just to keep them tuned in when there's only three subs going to come in.* I was reasonably relaxed.

In the dressing room, though, Charlie started powering us up. Mikey Sheehy (a god of Kerry football, a gentleman, and someone who was to become a great friend of mine) was a selector and was walking around talking to each player, lads were getting togged, going through their individual rituals, whatever those were, and Charlie was hammering it home: the jersey, and what it meant, and what we were about, and who we were representing, and to be honest the heart was nearly coming out of my chest by the time he was done.

The door burst open and out we went.

Because Kerry were playing in the senior semi-final afterwards against Kildare, there was a decent crowd in for the minor game, but of course the first thing that came into my head was, *My family are here somewhere looking at me.*

When the ball was kicked to me in the warm-up I was nearly going 10 feet off the ground to field it. Every kick was crisp, every hand-pass accurate – but at the same time I'd glance into the crowd the odd time.

As I say, because I wasn't starting I didn't feel that pressure. As we were coming in on the bus I'd have gone through the three most likely lads to come on, and why they were likely to come on, and I didn't put myself in that group. So as far as I was concerned, I could just relax and watch the game.

About 10 minutes into the second half, though, I heard

a shout: 'Aidan O'Mahony, warm up.' It didn't sink in at all. I had to be told a second time, and even then I was shocked.

I also didn't know what to do to warm up, to be honest.

There was a big following up from Rathmore and Glenflesk to see Declan O'Keeffe, John Crowley and Séamus Moynihan in the senior game, and they must have been near to where I was warming up (by which I mean just running up and down the sideline) because I heard them roaring at me as I ran up and down. It got pretty real then, and that encouragement was refreshing.

I was thinking, *Who's coming off and where am I going?*, and then it happened. I had to go over to the linesman. He put his hand on my back and said, 'You'll be going on there in a minute.'

Charlie told me who to mark and to get on the ball, and I was out there.

It was like a dream come true, but I was soon in the thick of it. I actually won a ball early on and – maybe because I was used to the speed of club football – within a second the ball was stripped off me by a Laois player.

I won it back and gave it off, but I knew immediately it was a completely different level to what I'd been used to.

Back then because a warm-up meant running up and down the sideline or kicking out the ankles and re-tying the laces a couple of times, getting up to the tempo of a full championship game was a real challenge. The speed of the game was a shock, no question about that, but the stakes were so high, I found myself forgetting to doubt myself. I was caught up in the game and my only focus then was the next ball.

Every time I touched the ball there was someone right on top of me – at times I was genuinely thinking, *Am I marking two different lads here or just one?* But as a defender, the job was to mark a man, win the ball, find a midfielder or beat it up to the half-forward line (based on the old-fashioned notion that if they couldn't win it themselves then they shouldn't be there in the first place).

There was a definite sense of unreality at times – at one stage I hit the ball down into Tadhg Kennelly and all I could see was white. All the Kildare support was in for the senior game already on Hill 16 and it was a wall of white from their jerseys. I can remember thinking it'd be hard to find the posts into that end.

The noise was another thing: if you won the ball there was a huge roar, and then if you got turned over or gave it away there was another roar, and then it went on again and again, the noise rising and falling in volume, up and down.

We were down a couple of points and we hit the post and the bar late on but eventually time ran out. Laois had won the game.

I stayed out on the pitch for a couple of extra minutes, just to soak it in, but when I came back into the dressing room it was my first real experience of what a loss is. The quietness. The collapse.

It has stayed with me, that sense of all the work that everyone had put in to get to that point suddenly gone. All year, all that work, but now it was over – and because it was minor, and most of the players would be overage by next year, there was no chance to make amends.

A minor team probably never gets together again after its last match. It comes together for a few months and then it breaks up, and even though I'd missed a few weeks with the broken nose – and was shy enough to wonder where to sit on the bus – we'd trained together and become a team. That's no small thing.

Down the line some lads move abroad, or to different parts of the country, or they drop out of football for whatever reason. So the day, and the defeat, is actually more significant than it seems at first, particularly to naive 18-year-olds.

The immediate impact of the defeat hits you first, though, and you don't want to experience it again. Seeing your pals crying in the dressing room. Seeing Charlie Nelligan and Mikey Sheehy – legends who'd won absolutely everything in the game – going around trying to console lads, but their shoulders slumped with the disappointment, disappointment that was 100 per cent felt for the players.

The county board chairman came in and said a few words, then we put on the tracksuits and walked out into the Hogan stand. Thankfully, people were good to us. Kerry supporters came over and shook hands and wished us well.

Then the Kerry and Kildare seniors came out for their semi-final. That definitely set something off in me. These were serious athletes, the crowd stood up for them, you had the ongoing show on the sideline between Mick O'Dwyer and Páidí Ó Sé ...

I was watching in awe. I got so wrapped up in the senior game I nearly forgot we'd lost our own match.

I was looking at some lads that I'd have come up against for the club a few weeks previously, but here in Croke Park those players looked like completely different human beings.

Still, I couldn't help but ask myself the obvious question: Could I survive out there? Could I be part of that?

Now, I also looked at the numbers. I was number 20-odd and had played 15 or 20 minutes on a losing minor team, but I'd been out there, at least. I'd played. I'd made that progress.

There was a benefit to not being obsessed with the jersey either. I was never under pressure to make it onto the minor team: there was never any 'His father or his brother played for Kerry, he'll have to match up.'

That never arose, and because of that I looked on the minor setup as an honour for me, not a step on the ladder. There was no pathway through the development squad system – because there was no development squad system – so the trials were old-fashioned. If you went to a trial and you were better than your man, you were in; if not, you were back to the club.

That helped me because there was no real sense of disappointment after I broke my nose in training – I knew I'd be going back to the club because that's how things were done, but having been in there once, I felt I had a chance of making it back there again.

Kildare won, so we all went back to Kerry together, minors and seniors, back to Revelles nightclub in Killarney – still wearing the polo shirt to remind us who we were and to remind everyone we met who we were. I didn't even drink at the time, so I was like a lark when my parents dropped down to collect me.

And that's another great memory that I have. When they pulled in for me, the pride was coming off them in waves. They told me they'd gone back to Rathmore after the game and gone down to the local, where people were coming up to them to congratulate them because I'd got on for a few minutes, telling them that it was great for the club.

As if I wasn't emotional enough after hearing that, I then noticed what was on the back seat: the letter I'd got from the county board telling me I was on the panel. Obviously my dad had been looking at it all week. The programme from the game was next to it.

To be honest, part of me wanted to cry right there in the back of the car.

I had Beano's Laois jersey in the bag and the football boots which still had grass stains from Croke Park. And I had the Kerry gear in there, which was more important to me than a medal at that moment.

The funny thing is, 1998 wouldn't stay in the memory for playing Kerry minor as much as for winning the junior county final with the club after that. It had been almost 30 years since we'd won the junior championship, and later in the year we came up against Finuge in the final.

That was some battle in Austin Stack Park. I ended up tangling with a young lad from Finuge and spent more time wrestling with him on the ground and bouncing off him than anything else: Paul Galvin was his name.

We went down to 14 men in the first half and had an uphill battle ahead of us. Finuge had Galvin, Éamonn Fitzmaurice, Éamonn Breen, the Corridans. It was a massive battle; the game wound down to a free Finuge needed to score in order to level the game, but they worked a short one and the referee blew it up. We'd won.

Looking back over an entire career, winning All-Irelands with Kerry stands out – the hype, the crowds, the focus. But that evening, coming back to Rathmore, past bonfire after bonfire, the hall packed with people, grown men crying and hugging each other … that was special.

Seamus Cooper, the trainer, was talking about the laps

we'd done and about getting John Buckley – our six-foot-six midfielder and always a man to saunter his way through training – to win the last of the 20 sprints we would do in a night; the kinds of yarns that every team tells the night they win a cup, the kind of fun you get out of being on a team.

I'd seen something in Croke Park that I wanted, but I also saw something in the club that I wanted. I'd fallen in from the soccer club early in the year to play a bit of football, but then in the middle of Austin Stack Park in November I'd played alongside a man who was in tears at the final whistle because he was nearly 20 years trying to win the competition we'd just captured.

That night in the community hall there were people from the locality that I'd never met coming up to shake hands and tell me how important the win was for the club and the area. The next morning we did the rounds of the schools with the cup, with small children waving up and cheering at the team.

That was a different level to Kerry but it was so important for us in Rathmore, that win. It was local, focused, and it would always be one of my greatest achievements and a springboard that would drive me on to further success.

Going forward it was all about accommodating my two passions, Kerry and Rathmore.

Another challenge. Another lesson learned.

The minor grade was my introduction to elite-level football, and from the first minute to the last, doubt was always present – I doubted my body would hold up due to asthma; I doubted my ability; before every game I'd create more doubt by naming the team out in my head – without taking a starting place for myself.

If I stripped the doubt out, and instead used that time to focus on my game, focus on the positives, visualise what I was going to do well, would this have led to a better performance overall?

I'd transitioned from a player who had only just started out with his club team to featuring in an All-Ireland semi-final. It wasn't until that was pointed out to me that I started to have some self-belief.

Back then I wasn't mature enough to stop the negative thinking, but now I combat doubt by using positives as motivation and by preparing thoroughly to ensure that all areas are covered.

3

Pushing the Boundaries

Hard Lessons at Under-21

I brought a certain amount of confidence into the under-21 grade. Not a sense of entitlement by any means: I'd played 20 minutes of one game as a minor substitute; I wasn't an established player with a string of performances to point to.

But a couple of things fell my way. For one thing Rathmore joined in with East Kerry at under-21 level, and the following year we went on to win the county final against West Kerry in Austin Stack Park.

There was a lot of quality on show in that game: West Kerry had the pick of An Gaeltacht and Dingle, so it was a good final to win.

And it was a good shop window for me. Same for a lot of players, but my attitude at the time was: *I'm*

playing corner-back, not full- or centre-back, so I'm not
as influential as other players.

I'd had a taste of the county scene with the minors and
felt that, to be in with a chance of the under-21 team, I'd
need to be playing in a central position at that level, and
in some ways I was right. I had under-21 trials in 1999
but I didn't make the cut.

Jack O'Connor was the manager, someone who'd
feature prominently in my career in years to come.
With the under-21s there wouldn't be much interaction
between you and the manager because it's basically a
question of trials and then training, and at the time Jack
had a very good crop of players coming through. Any
manager would have his team nearly picked before the
season even began. But the fact that he called me into the
trial games, even, was encouraging. Despite that short
appearance for the county minors, when Jack put me in a
trial for the under-21s I could say to myself, *Well, he sees*
me in the top 30-odd players in the county at this grade
and there are three years in it for me.

I knew I had work to do. I was too light. My fitness
levels weren't up to scratch either. Going deeper, there
were two different trajectories involved for the players:
a lot of these lads had their eye on getting themselves a
Kerry senior jersey. I had my eye on an under-21 jersey.

As a comparison, I was looking at players like Tom
O'Sullivan, a club-mate of mine, someone who had such

natural pace that he'd glide through games: someone who would annihilate his man with pure speed. Other players were well-built, well-conditioned, and they were clearly ready for the senior inter-county scene.

The difference for me at the time was that I wasn't taking that on board. Even though I was marking inter-county forwards at club level with Rathmore, I wasn't noticing those different requirements: after a game I wasn't thinking, *I could live with that guy football-wise but he's very strong, very well-conditioned, and I'm going to have to get to the same level.*

If I went into under-21 training and picked up someone like Noel Kennelly, who played like a senior player (and went on to play for the senior squad) – he had adapted, he knew where he wanted to go, whereas I was off the pace.

Also, I was an out-and-out defender, a man-marker with the club. If I wasn't seen, that was fine because it meant my man wasn't being seen either, so in my mind that was job done. And at the beginning, that certainly suited me.

But these guys at the top level were doing the man-marking job at the back and then contributing more besides. They were getting up and down the field to help out the forwards and chip in with a score the odd time. Stephen O'Sullivan and Marc Ó Sé were flying up and down the field; other guys like Tom O'Sullivan, Michael McCarthy, Tomás Ó Sé, they were helping out at both ends of the field as well, not just blotting out an opponent.

Eventually that under-21 team made the All-Ireland final, and even though Westmeath beat them, they still had future household names playing that day, fellas who would give years to the Kerry senior team.

That was the learning curve at inter-county level but my confidence was growing at club level at least. East Kerry won the Kerry senior county championship, so that was building me up ahead of 2000.

I was also learning from the college scene. I was in Cork Institute of Technology (CIT) and though I hadn't played freshers football there, I fell in with the Sigerson Cup panel in my second year because I knew well that people often said playing third-level was the next best thing to senior inter-county.

Keith Ricken and Liam Hodnett were over the team, and it was a good one – Graham Canty, Derek Kavanagh, Alan Cronin, lads who were playing with the Cork seniors.

That helped, and so did the calendar. I was called into the Kerry under-21 for trials, did well with Rathmore, won a county with East Kerry, and trained and played with CIT. Those commitments all ran into each other and were complementing each other – I was learning, growing and gaining knowledge of the game, management and players.

John Evans took over the Kerry under-21s for 2000. We all knew about his record with the great Laune Rangers team that won the All-Ireland club title in 1996 – and he told us about that, about what it was like to bring a team from scratch to an All-Ireland club title. That was a long journey and it wasn't an easy one at times.

He was a great character, but for us those kinds of stories were a great motivation as well. We were left thinking, *If he can do that with a club team, what'll he do with this team?* The under-21s had narrowly lost an All-Ireland the year before, after all.

I was on the panel of 24 at least for 2000, so my focus moved to winning a place on the starting 15. John was good with young players; he was supportive, good to put an arm around the shoulder and give some positive feedback, some valuable direction. For instance, we had a lot of racehorses in that group – Billy Sheehan, John Sugrue and I have a vivid memory of doing rounds of the small pitch at the back of Fitzgerald stadium.

We heard, 'Stretch!', which meant flat to the mat, then being sent left, being sent right – doing the runs in twos and hanging on for dear life, literally.

Again, it was a test of our mental toughness, to see if you had the stomach for the challenge – I was praying silently, *Say left*, because at least I was on the inside lane for the run, and he'd say, 'Go right', knowing well I would be going the scenic route.

That could go on for 20 or 25 minutes. Looking over at Evans, he could be pouring water out on the grass and saying out loud, 'We don't need any water.' At that stage I'd be thinking, *You're right, it's a miracle I need, not water*. It was pure hardship to toughen players.

Some lads are built for running. They're always out at the head of the pack, leading and not following.

I should have been cuter and hung around the middle of the pack, but any player worth his salt wants to impress the manager. I found the running very tough because nobody ever told me, 'Hang in there and get your second wind, you'll be grand' – and also because the asthma was another fallback, another excuse.

I'd be hanging on for dear life at the back of the group. Now, if I put on a manager's hat for a second, my view of a player like that would be, *This guy is barely surviving, barely hanging in there – what'll he be like in the melting pot of a Munster final with 10 minutes left?* That's the reality of the game, the reality of how managers view players.

The bottom line was that I wasn't progressing. The other lads were getting fitter and stronger. I was just surviving. Hanging in there.

That wasn't good enough. Some of the lads in the under-21 squad had been in with the Kerry seniors and had experienced training at another level of hardship again. For me, I was coming in from the college scene, which had a lot to recommend it, but which also had one flaw.

A few county players on a college team could nearly carry that team, and often did – the likes of Graham Canty could do something in a game that could flip it on its head totally, which meant you only had to focus on doing your own job. Not a bad situation to be in during a particular game, but not something that would help you to advance your career either.

John Evans would have felt that if he had a full team, with no injuries, he'd go a long way towards winning an All-Ireland.

As it turned out, we drew with Waterford in the first round of the Munster championship. I was a sub that day but didn't get on. The game was notable for the first-ever appearance of a kicking tee, used by our keeper Donnacha Enright – though I think it was a plastic 7-Up bottle cut in two, which the umpire fired out over the wire at one stage anyway.

The 15 that drew with Waterford were given a chance to redeem themselves in the replay. Most if not all of them started in that game – and Waterford beat us.

That was a tough dressing room to be in. With all due respect to Waterford, we were in Killarney, and there's an expectation when the Kerry jersey goes on that All-Irelands are in the picture. That's not an arrogance, it's just the expectation, the demand, the high standards that are expected.

I think most squad players who don't participate in a

game like that feel hard done by personally. Those players feel they could have done something.

I was massively disappointed. My thinking was, *Well, I'll hardly play senior for Kerry if I was just a panellist on the under-21 team that Waterford beat in Killarney.*

The irony is that a few of those lads had long careers as Kerry seniors, but I was disillusioned at that stage. Twenty minutes as a minor, I didn't make the under-21 panel the first year, and was a sub the second year when they lost to Waterford – and I'd found that the training was brutally hard all the way along.

The mindset becomes very negative in that scenario. It's easy to get lost in it. However, deep down my determination, commitment and passion were still there.

The upside? It was Rathmore's first year playing senior after winning the intermediate championship in 1999. That was major for the club, a huge positive. For Rathmore, for the locality, and for myself it was fantastic – going from junior club status in 1998, after waiting nearly 29 years to win that championship, then winning the intermediate championship in our first year there. And now, 2000, Rathmore were at the top table. A senior team.

That was part of the reason, turning into 2001, that I had a serious think about myself and where I was going. I asked myself some hard questions, including: Why had certain players made it onto the Kerry under-21 team and I hadn't?

The answer I came up with was because they were up the front in the running. They were leading it out. To get on with Kerry you just had to lead it out, and the first night back in with the Kerry under-21s, my last year at the grade, I was up the front in the running.

I was capable of this: that's what I kept telling myself. I knew I had to get myself up to the front, that it was easier to be up there dictating the pace than hanging on at the back. It was achievable.

The format was the same: 'stretch', 'go left', 'go right' – and I kept saying to the rest of them, 'Don't give in, don't give in.' I knew Evans could hear me, and a bit of bite came into it, I could tell. He was talking about running the Laune Rangers guys and the 'older players' training in that group: 'They were saying not to give in either, but I ran them for 40 minutes.' I kept on with the 'Don't give in' to the rest of the lads in return, and we carried on running. And eventually we stopped.

After training we fell in for a meeting, the first of 2001.

And John said, 'Last year Aidan O'Mahony was down the back of the runs and didn't make the team, but this year he's up the front.'

That always stuck with me, a lesson that left its mark. If you want to be part of something, to really be central to it, then you have to lead. That's not a casual comment. If I put 2000 and 2001 next to each other as parallel seasons, the differences are obvious.

In 2000 I wanted to be there but I didn't want to put in the hard yards. In 2001 I wanted it but I put in the hard yards.

There was a captaincy there to be won as well, and I wasn't using excuses. When the training was severe in January and February then the asthma was severe, but you can break that barrier and get out the other side. I had realised that it was all about mindset.

Being up the front alongside Eoin Brosnan, Seán O'Sullivan and Marc Ó Sé for the runs was refreshing and rewarding, but it also made me review my own attitude: why didn't I have more faith in myself and pick teams with myself on them?

That showed me my mindset had changed totally. My attitude, my sense of pride – they were all far better.

Ambrose O'Donovan from Gneeveguilla and Tom O'Connor from Kenmare were with the team management. Super characters. If there was a dust-up in training, Ambrose would be stoking that in the car on the way home.

You can imagine the effect that would have on a young fella, hearing it from a god that had brought Sam Maguire to Gneeveguilla.

Evans was the main man, though. He trained us very hard again that year, and this time the positives from that were clearer to me.

Yes, you must have the skills no matter what sport you're playing, but everything comes from fitness. The confidence, the belief, all of that goes into the pot with your skills and your fitness, and your entire performance moves up a level as a result. I was progressing and I was content with it.

At the time CIT and UCC were having great clashes at college level as well – Paul Galvin, Ian Twiss and Michael Cahill were playing for UCC, and from a player's point of view you were competing against top inter-county performers on the college scene week in, week out.

On the club scene East Kerry and Mid Kerry drew the under-21 county final, and I was East Kerry captain.

Because Kerry were out in the Munster under-21 championship soon enough afterwards, the county final replay was postponed. Seán O'Sullivan was Mid Kerry captain so it came down to the two of us and I got the nod as captain of Kerry.

Evans rang me to give me the news, and in all honesty after he said the word 'captain', everything else was basically a blur. It didn't sink in at all. He also told me I'd be the centre-back. It would be my first start in a Kerry jersey.

For my parents it was wonderful, and going into CIT the following day, it was a big deal as well. Graham Canty was Cork under-21 captain and I'd played with him and a lot of the other Cork lads also with the college.

That was a significant part of the equation too, living in Cork, though not for the traditional rivalry. After a hard training session in Killarney, you might make the last hour in Gorby's, a nightclub in Cork we were all fond of.

A week and a half before the game, though, after training on the Thursday I headed straight to the student house in Uam Var Drive near the college.

We were relaxing away the following morning, playing FIFA on the Xbox, when I noticed the screen beginning to blur. The next thing I saw were fluorescent jackets: I was on a stretcher being carried out the door by paramedics, with my neighbour from next door leaning over to ask me if I was alright.

When the lads from the house came in to see me later that day in the Mercy hospital they said I'd had a seizure on the couch.

I was asking who'd won the game on the Xbox and Moss O'Keeffe told me I'd sneaked it. But obviously I was worried, particularly with the game coming up: I'm in hospital after a seizure and yet in just over a week I'm supposed to captain Kerry against Cork in a football game?

On one level I was thinking, *Is starting a game for Kerry going to happen for me at all?* The doubts aren't long coming into your head and I began to blame myself for not minding myself properly.

Being on my own in the bed in hospital didn't help either. I was emotional, feeling sorry for myself, and then the doctor came in and said my blood sugar was low – only for me to bring up the game the following week.

He was laughing, telling me to look after my health first. He said if the blood sugars came back up to what they were supposed to be then they could consider what the options were, but all that was in my head was the game, pure and simple.

That was a Friday, and a specialist eventually came in to say my blood sugars were improving and I might be let home that Sunday.

The Sunday came, though, and when they tested me the blood sugars were low again. By then I was coming up with all sorts of reasons for the low sugar levels – including the lack of sugar in the bread I was eating in the hospital.

John Evans was in touch that day to see how I was. There was no discussion of the game and being right for it, but he said they'd be training on the Tuesday night.

I told him I'd be out that evening, Sunday, and that I'd see him on the Tuesday. He said to mind myself, he'd see me then.

I was telling the truth: I'd been told I'd be discharged that Sunday. But then another issue popped up. I was told by the Kerry county board that in order to play the following weekend, I needed to get a letter from the doctors authorising that, clearing me to play.

When the specialist came in for a word before I left, he was saying that I was training too hard, studying, travelling, maybe not eating properly, and that all these things had come together, and that I'd have to be careful …

Now, in my head I was hardly listening. I was thinking, *I'm in the shape of my life. I'm ready for the game next Sunday.*

'Have you any questions for me?' he said eventually.

'I do,' I said. 'Will you just write out a note for me that I'm allowed to play next week, that everything's fine?'

'I can't do that.'

I thought for a second he hadn't heard what I said, so I actually just repeated myself word for word.

'No,' he said. 'We don't know the exact reason for what happened. Something caused you to have low blood sugars and I can't sign off on that.'

I left, went back to my digs to pick up my gear and headed home to recover.

It was a strange time. I was drained after the experience and the few days in hospital, not sleeping properly with all the thoughts of the game – not to mention the man on the panel who might come into the team instead of me and wondering what to do next.

John Evans rang and asked me how I was, and I explained to him that the specialist hadn't signed off. John told me his hands were tied, that he couldn't play me in those circumstances.

I was so desperate, I tried to convince him that the specialist had no interest in football, so how could he know what he was talking about. A specialist! But John, understandably enough, said that although I could train with the team and travel to the game with them, without medical clearance I couldn't play. That was a chance they couldn't take.

Eventually I hit on a plan. I asked my father to drop me to another doctor.

I put my case to him and told him I felt fine, that I had training the following night and I needed to be signed off as healthy to train and to represent Rathmore, and Kerry, the following weekend. I had it all prepared in advance, all the emotional manipulation I could come up with, and after my extensive and persuasive explanation, he signed off on me playing.

The following night I was togged off and ready before I even landed into Killarney for training.

The letter from the doctor was like a Visa card in a student's pocket. I walked in and unfolded it for John, said nothing and went out training. We trained on the Thursday and the team was announced to the media, with me captain and starting at centre-back.

Before the Cork game I spoke in the dressing room, the first time I ever spoke to a group. In one way it's a good thing there are no recordings of it because, at the time, little preparation was invested in those speeches.

However, young lads have a different approach anyway; they just want to go out and play.

When we got out onto the pitch in Páirc Uí Chaoimh I continued my old routine from club games: watching the man I was on to get an idea of what leg he favoured, how he moved and doing all my pre-analysis.

There were plenty of butterflies in the stomach. I had a few pokers in that fire – Rathmore being so close to Cork, captaining the team, knowing so many of the Cork lads from CIT – but there was another level of responsibility in being captain.

Going up for the toss of the coin, I saw that there was a big crowd there, with a good share from Rathmore.

A guy I was in college with, Ollie Favier from Glenflesk, was a sub that day, and I'd say Glenflesk and Rathmore between them sent two buses up because we were involved that evening.

We won the toss but lost the game. By a point.

Declan Quill was outstanding for us that evening: he must have hit five points from play. We were close, we hit the post and the crossbar a couple of times, but we went down by 1–12 to 1–11.

Coming into the dressing room I was feeling down, naturally enough. When we drew Cork we were thinking, *Beat them and we have a good chance of winning the Munster title and maybe going further*. It's only human nature to let yourself dream about that a little, bringing the cup back to Rathmore. It's a kid's mentality but a positive one.

I remember, though, when John Evans spoke so passionately in the dressing room it made me realise just how much work he and the management team had put into us, all that effort, and then I felt sorrier for them after losing than for myself. We had trained so hard and prepared well, and they had facilitated all of that. Now it was gone.

There was another lesson on the way back. Another stepping-stone. I was in a car with John Evans and Ambrose O'Donovan along with Ollie and Eoin Brosnan, and we stopped off in Ballyvourney on the way home.

And that was another big difference, being together as adults having a drink, rather than – as you have with minors – kids and adults in two separate groups.

The game was over with, we'd done our best and left it all out there, so fellas were entitled to a beer. That was a different outlook.

I think that night was actually Ollie's birthday, so we stopped at his house in Glenflesk to see his father Dan. Our ultimate aim was the nightspots of Killarney, of course, young lads eager to get out, but when we stopped at the Favier house Dan made a great welcome for us, and for John Evans.

The kettle was put on, and the chat started, and though we were still fairly keen on getting to Killarney, Dan brought out a bottle of whiskey and a few glasses just to mix things up. Now, the whiskey wasn't shared equally, because the colour of the liquid got lighter as you went around the table.

John and Ambrose had glasses which were nice and dark, while myself, Eoin and Ollie's glasses were practically transparent, which was probably just as well. But the camaraderie and the fun involved was unforgettable. It underlined that the journey was for everyone – not just the players but also the management team, the entire collective.

No stone had been left unturned and we had given it our best shot: we came up just short, but the most powerful memory is of that journey back down the road with my team-mates, and Killarney, which we made eventually that night to celebrate Ollie's birthday with the rest of the panel.

We met up again the following day, but that was the finish of that group. Like the minors, we were all going in different directions and we wouldn't be together again, but it was a milestone for me.

I'd captained Kerry and picked up a few valuable lessons. I got player of the year with Rathmore, which was a fantastic honour and gave my self-confidence a boost too.

At 21 I was at a crossroads in my football career, though. I was out of the underage grades, and senior inter-county was the mountain left to climb.

I had three years at under-21 level – from making the grade through trials in year one, making the bench in year two, and then as captain in the third year. The person in year three was completely different to the person starting out.

As captain, I had to lead from the front, first in everything, constantly. That year made me push the boundaries and take my preparation to another level, week after week. All the way through to the end of the season, everything was carried out to my absolute best: my routine during the day; nutrition; even after games we won, my focus was straight back to recovery, to tomorrow's training session, nutrition. It was full-on.

The biggest eye-opener for me was when my final under-21 game finished up and it was time to hand the (imaginary) armband back: my overall game had been taken to another level; my general life skills, my organisation, my structure, my drive and my focus were constant. Why now should I stop this level of consistency?

4

Pushing Past My Boundaries
Senior Breakthrough

Leaving under-21 is a little bit like leaving home for the first time. There's no-one around any more holding your hand. It's down to yourself.

Rathmore moving to the senior grade meant we broke away from playing with the East Kerry divisional side, which meant in turn that I had more responsibility in club games – and a bigger shop window for a potential Kerry call-up in championship games. I was playing centre-back and midfield, and my fitness levels were very high, so high that I was able to take on more of a leadership role in the team.

Taking on more responsibility with the club was a positive. I was enjoying being part of that club ethos that only the players in the group know about. The lads you train with and go to war alongside all have to buy into it, and with Rathmore we had a tight group.

The gym culture was non-existent at that stage in Gaelic games. My own strength was a combination effect of the extensive work on the farm and other physical labour and my own individual fitness work.

That was bringing my own game to a whole new level, but – and there's always a 'but' – my pace would have been questioned. I know that players doubted my speed: 'He's very strong, a good fielder, he can mix it, but is he short a yard? Does he have the pace?'

My strengths were as a man-marker, defending hard, but to take the next step – the crucial step to the highest rung on the ladder – you need more.

And once you leave under-21 you know you're not a kid any more, that it's up to you to make that leap. It doesn't seem so long ago looking back – although it's still 20 years – but sports science wasn't really a factor then.

It wasn't a case of looking up the specific exercises – drills, plyometrics – and making them part of your regime to add pace at team training sessions.

It was down to the player to figure it out for himself.

We had a very strong club team at the time, and I was usually in midfield. Along with many of the players on that Rathmore team, I learned pretty fast what you needed to do to survive.

Gaelic football is a game that demands skill and fitness, but you need to have that extra mental drive and toughness if you want to bring your game to another level.

I was at a stage where I could apply the lessons I'd learned in club games. I knew I had to make a mark and often I was playing against county players, guys who were well established with Kerry.

If I kept one of them scoreless in a game, though, I'd be thinking, *Hang on here, what am I doing wrong? Does Páidí not see something in me, something that I could add to Kerry?*

Páidí was Páidí Ó Sé, who was manager of Kerry at the time. I thought there might be a call to come in to Kerry training at some stage in 2002, but no. The phone stayed silent.

But at the end of that year, the call came.

At first I thought it was one of the lads from college pretending to be Páidí, just to wind me up, but it was actually the man himself.

This was Páidí – the man who'd won everything, captained Kerry to All-Irelands, managed Kerry to All-Irelands – on the other end of the line.

We had a game against Ballymacelligott that weekend and Páidí said he'd be going to it, just to watch me. Grand.

Afterwards I asked one of the Rathmore lads if he'd seen Páidí at the game.

No: no sign of him.

I spent the trip home wondering if that was positive or negative – did he have his mind made up to bring me in or had he given up on me already?

Then, another phone call from him.

He mentioned that I was a man-marker, that that was what I did well.

On the other side of the conversation I was trying to get a message across: 'I'm picking up the main players on the opposing teams all the time.'

Of course, he was getting another message entirely back to me: 'Hey, the main players are all inside here with me in Kerry, training, and they're a different calibre.'

But he spelt it out. He said if there was a graph, the lads with Kerry were at the top and I was coming along but I was still in the middle. I needed to add more to my game.

Then at the end of the call he said, 'Are you still playing that soccer?'

Another message.

'I am,' I said.

'Well, it's one or the other,' he said.

I took the lesson on board. What he was really saying was that I was already playing on too many teams, between Rathmore and the college, and as a result I wasn't realising my potential with any of them.

I also had my own motivations. At the time I was working in Billy Morgan's bar in Cork – Keith Ricken of CIT, a great coach and mentor, had helped me to get a job there – and I was working there during the Munster final of 2002.

That day the Rathmore crowd came into the bar in huge numbers – they were all up to support Declan O'Keeffe and Tom O'Sullivan, who were playing that day for Kerry against Cork.

My brother Kieran and a few others had come up on the Saturday night, and they had come in for food before the match, with yours truly behind the bar, serving them. I wasn't going to the game myself – I was working for the afternoon.

After a certain point there was complete silence in the bar. They'd all left, heading to the Páirc to support the local heroes; they'd made all their plans for the weekend around being there to support them.

I never forgot that. It made a huge impression on me, the fact that everything was organised around supporting the lads. They all came back to the bar afterwards for a drink, Tom included, and I noticed the pride they had in him, having represented Rathmore as well as Kerry.

Tom was a few years ahead of me in Shrone school and grew up to be one of the best man-markers in Gaelic football, never mind in Kerry.

At club level it was insane – if you wanted an opposing forward to disappear out of a game, never to be seen from start to finish, Tom just took over. He marked the forward out of it and made it look easy.

I knew in my mind I was at a crossroads. I'd received two calls from the main man in Kerry and it was in my hands.

I decided to move home to Kerry, cut the travelling and make football my priority.

I was in and out of the senior setup for trials and so on, and eventually I got called in for the final league game against Armagh.

The team was down a few defenders through injury, and I remember thinking – with a bit of a start – that I was in with a chance of a game. More importantly, I had my foot in the door and I knew I was ready to work once I got the call.

If players are honest, they have two different stories. To your friends and family and the general public you're saying, 'Yeah, really looking forward to this, it's going to be great,' but in your heart you're aware of the reality. I could remember the adjustment needed for Kerry under-21 training, for instance, and I knew certain players on that team had gone on ahead of me to a different level of conditioning.

So the mindset the player himself has is different. Once you get past the joy of having the Kerry senior shorts and socks, you realise the seriousness of the situation.

The warm-up for that league game in Tralee was at a level I was not accustomed to. It was serious. Kerry needed to get a win that day, while Armagh were still one of the top teams. It was a time when only three subs could be brought on during a game, and I knew well I wouldn't be one of them.

I didn't feature in the Armagh game but I knew what was coming down the line for the next few weeks.

After that match, though, I can remember a conversation with Eddie 'Tatler' O'Sullivan, who was a selector. He said most of the established Kerry players were going to fall back in with their clubs, which was the done thing at the time – after the league wrapped up, most of the lads played with the clubs for a few weeks.

'But we'll have three or four weeks of hard training for lads that need to get up to the level of the others,' he said. Actually, 'really hard training' was the description he used. Eddie was an East Kerry man and was keeping an eye out for another East Kerry man. I would form a great bond with Eddie for years after and also with his son Patrick, who would play a huge part in my career as chairman of the Kerry county board.

Eddie was telling me, in effect, that even as a young fella there was a great opportunity there for me if I focused myself. I needed to go through the hard yards to do so.

If I didn't want that, I could go away and enjoy life in college and play with the club. But if I did want it, then I had to commit to it, all out.

That I did. That was a Sunday, and on Tuesday we started a block of training on the sand-based pitch in Dr

Crokes in Killarney under the watchful eye of the Kerry trainer, John O'Keeffe, a man who I have admired all my career.

I'll never forget those first four nights. 'Really hard training' was a fair description.

Paul Kennedy, who was one of the group, was an unbelievable athlete. Paul led out the running at a very high tempo, and during the first lap I was going back to my mantra for surviving savage training sessions, telling myself, *Hang on in the middle for dear life.*

That training was unforgettable. Full-on, flat to the floor, run, run, run – no recoveries were integrated, legs were burning, head spinning and the lungs were fit to burst. And then repeat.

A week went by. A second week. And I found I was moving up. Eddie Tatler rang me to confirm it: he said I was progressing very well.

Eddie was another person who helped me climb that ladder by seeing something in me and pushing me past my own limits. I had Seamus Cooper in my corner with Rathmore and Eddie in the Kerry setup.

Looking back, I'd say the Kerry management responded to my appetite for punishment, how I kept coming back and back. They may have been thinking, *This guy could be a rough diamond. If we can only polish him ...*

At the time I was flicking between college and working for Dawn Dairies on the road – up at 4.30 in the morning, heading back to west Kerry delivering dairy products. I was also considering applying to the Garda College. Becoming a guard was something I'd always wanted to do – a job that would enable me to give something back to the community, and also one where I would leave the house every morning not knowing what was ahead of me, which really appealed to me.

It was a great time in my life, travelling the county, but I was also living the life of a county player, where your body has to be an absolute temple.

The downside was that I was getting light. There was so much running in the sessions that I was burning off calories the whole time, and that was the beginning of me going to the gym.

I was starting as a complete beginner, with no-one to advise me on how to use the bar and build up, but I knew I had to do something. I was too light and had to begin building myself up and increasing the power.

That showed me something else. That I'd crossed a threshold in terms of what I wanted out of the entire experience. It wasn't enough for me just to be there and holding down a spot in the dressing room. I wanted to lead.

But by the time of the Munster final against Limerick I remember sitting alongside Paul Galvin on the bench and my attitude was completely different. *I'm able for that now*, I thought, *I should be in there, and I want to be in there*. I had no time for any self-doubt.

That was what the block of hard training did for me. Getting through those hard sessions built that confidence; I had been able to get up to the front of the runs with the likes of the Mac Gearailts. If we started off with three laps of the field absolutely flat out, I was able to stay up the front, without a problem.

In the games in training I was able to mark my man, and a number of times I'd chance a dart up the field without a challenge.

Páidí wouldn't be long shouting at me to get back on my man. At first I was thinking, *What does he want from me? I'm marking my man solid and I'm increasing my confidence with runs up the field as well.*

But it took me a while to realise they wanted me to mark my man and not to be sprinting up the field. It was a different game back then, but if that's what was required, that's what I was going to deliver.

My asthma wasn't a factor as much because the jersey consumed me, mind and body. Simple as that. On the Tuesday night before the first championship game in 2003 against Tipperary, which Kerry would win and go on to play Limerick in the Munster Final, Páidí told me I was on the panel but not to tell anyone, which was a fair challenge for me.

Everything comes to those who wait, though. A brown envelope arrived to the house with the news. Very official.

In a house that only bought one newspaper, that day my parents decided to get six of them, because the name was there in each one of them, in black and white: No. 24 A. O'Mahony (Rathmore).

Again, it really made them proud, and that in turn made me proud. I was in a privileged position, and I knew it.

In that Munster final Stephen Kelly, who I would work with later in the gardaí, was superb for Limerick. He had a background in rugby and had great upper-body strength and pace – he was breaking tackles and travelling with the ball, constantly driving at our defence.

And I was thinking to myself, *I should be in there marking him. I mightn't have his raw pace but I have the conditioning now for that. I'm strong, I've done the running and I want to be out there.*

Kerry won, and there were other things to enjoy. Going for a meal after the match, seeing Séamus Moynihan and Declan O'Keeffe sitting at a table, was great.

Out and about with the team afterwards for a drink was another experience. No Kerry branded tops, by the way. Casual clothes. Thinking back, that meant 30 lads all wearing boot-cut jeans.

After the Munster final we were back training but the team wasn't going to change. That wasn't how it was done – no matter how you were going in training, a player like me was serving his apprenticeship, really. I wanted to start but I was really there to sharpen up the player I was marking in training.

I took that seriously. Liam Hassett – or whoever – might hit me in training, and I'd give it right back to him to get him ready. That in itself was a change too, because before that I'd have been practically in awe looking at him.

Now I was on his toes, on other players' toes, pulling and dragging out of them, which was what they'd get in a game; they'd hop off me and I'd give it back. Testing, niggling, scratching away at them.

A lot of people don't understand that about inter-county training. It's on the edge all the time because it has to be to prepare lads for games. It's beyond competitive.

For someone like me at the time, the outlook was different. I was a panellist, not a player – I had a job to do within the panel and I was happy to do it, though if someone kicked two points off me at training it would be a long drive home afterwards as I stewed away.

The management probably saw me as being hard on myself with that attitude but they were also probably thinking, *He's raw but he's showing the right signs that he wants to play for Kerry.*

And I did. Sitting in a dressing room with Séamus Moynihan sitting across from you – what Kerry footballer wouldn't love that opportunity?

The benefits of the training and the attitude were

visible elsewhere as well. It was tough training with Kerry on Tuesday and Thursday. But come a club match on the Saturday? I was flying. Running flat out for 60 minutes was no problem.

I was conscious of my luck. In everything in life you need a break, and I had got mine.

Senior level was a whole new ball game. You learn what it means to earn that coveted cloth on your back: training is at a level you never imagined; every inch of your body and mind is being questioned with every blade of grass you cover.

There's no doubt in my mind now that to get through those hard yards – pushing my body to new limits I'd never imagined, never knew it could reach – I needed people who saw something in me that wasn't visible to my own eyes. I see now that I was a rough diamond waiting to be polished, being pushed to extreme levels so I could see who I could be, not who I thought I was.

Overcoming obstacles and boundaries was now part of who I was, and by exceeding my own expectations I was rewarding not only myself but also the people who had given me the help from day one.

5

A Stroke of Luck in Munster
on My Way to the Big One

If you're going to matches and watching players you can see what they bring to the table. In football it's all out there on the field in front of you, obviously enough. But if you're in a dressing room with a player you see a different side to them. Take someone like Séamus Moynihan: his ability was no secret; he was a majestic footballer from a very young age, that was clear to everyone. What you saw was what you got: he produced the goods every day, in every game.

But the first night I came into Kerry senior training he came over to have a chat and to make me feel welcome. After the session, hard as it was, he was over again to put a hand on the shoulder to encourage me.

Those are small things, but they last a lifetime because he's the one doing it – and obviously it's something I'd have done myself when I got older, to carry that on. His fielding. The way he carried the ball up the field. I'd seen him in games between Glenflesk and Rathmore – up close when I tried to put him on his backside in one of those games, as he often pointed out – but to see him prepare, his skills, his attitude, was an education. There was a player who could literally turn a game in a heartbeat.

He's good company as well on a night out. Plenty of roguery and good for a sing-song. But even in the middle of a session he'd be sure to have everyone involved, every player feeling part of the group.

In the chat with him, even having a drink after a game, the passion for football would come out of him. You'd nearly breathe it in from his conversation, what the GAA means, but for anyone having that conversation, myself included, there was something unreal about it. You're almost outside the conversation watching on: here you are and one of the best footballers in the country is talking to you about the game and asking how you're doing.

Séamus was a great man to tell you what you needed to be doing to get up to the level – not in a lecturing way, but as if the two of you were pals out for a chat. He'd talk to number 24 or 25 on the panel the same as the big stars, and make the same points to everyone.

When people talk about leaders on the pitch and off, that's the kind of person they mean, but it was just innate in Séamus. That's the kind of person he is.

It's the same when you're dealing with the Ó Sés. Marc was the one I knew best coming up because we were on the same underage teams, but the three of them, Darragh, Tomás and Marc, had an aura, particularly when they were all together. All six feet tall, the shoulders back and chests out, men who had gone to war for their county on the field but relaxed and easy-going off it.

Jack O'Connor took over as manager of Kerry in 2004, a different style of play, fresh faces being introduced to the panel and for every player a clean slate to prove what they could do if given the opportunity. I got my chance in the league, always trying to better myself in every game we played. I was consistent without being spectacular but I was rewarding Jack with the faith he had placed in me, growing in confidence with each league game I played in and believing I was ready to nail down a starting position come championship.

I was picked to start against Cork in the Munster semi-final. I was going to mark Colin Crowley, who was captain of Cork at the time, so it wasn't just about starting the game for Kerry: it was picking up the opposing team's captain.

Here's another change in the game since I started. Nowadays there wouldn't be as big a deal about that, given the systems and the way players switch in and out on each other, but back then it was significant if you were picking up your opponents' captain.

The game was huge for me. I was still living at home in Rathmore, so getting up that morning I had my parents for company over breakfast. They were more nervous for me than anything – but Cork versus Kerry in Killarney is always a massive day.

I can remember putting on the tracksuit early enough in the day and checking the big blue gear bag a dozen times to make sure everything was on board – the Adidas World Cup boots in particular.

I was collected by Tom O'Sullivan, which was a good move for a debutant because Tom was so laidback we might have been heading for a cup of coffee inside in Killarney rather than a Munster championship game. Completely relaxed.

We landed in to the old dressing rooms in Killarney but even before we got in the door the difference was clear. Tomás Ó Sé would have referred to the 'white heat' of a championship game, and he was absolutely right. The atmosphere is different immediately. There's a level of expectation that you can almost touch.

Even when the warm-up is taking place on Crokes' pitch, across the road from Fitzgerald stadium, the tension is building because the roars from the stadium for the minor game are drifting across. You're going back and forth, loosening out and stretching, and those roars are getting louder as more and more people filter through to the stadium.

Gladiators in the Colosseum? It's not an exaggeration. Cork and Kerry is like nothing else. It's just based on what we've seen over the years, the way the two counties have represented themselves in unbelievable battles.

That said, I never watched those games as a child thinking that I'd be involved myself one day. Did I want to be there? Yes. But when I got there I had a different question: Did I *really* want to be there?

It's not something you often hear from players, but I'd have second-guessed myself at that stage. I had plenty of negative thoughts: that I was too young, that I hadn't been tested, that this was a different level of football.

The game went well for me, and I'd give Jack O'Connor huge credit for that. As a manager he was one of the best to prepare you for a big game like that because he kept it simple beforehand: 'Go in there, mark your man, we don't need to see you as long as we don't see him.'

I learned a good bit that day, such as the importance of getting on the ball early, or getting a block in, or doing something that gets the crowd behind you, which builds your confidence. Every player needs that, and a newcomer more than most.

The way I would have approached that game mentally would have been along the lines of, 'I don't want to be the reason Kerry lose this game.' I'd have been conscious of being seen as a potential weak link in the defence – that other coaches would be thinking, *This lad is only starting off, we'll test his pulse early on.* I should have been more positive about myself, had more self-belief, but then when you factor in the prospect of picking up the opposing team's captain ...

All of this was rolling through my head at the very start of the game, when Colin came in and stood next to me. For the very first ball that came our way, he was about 20 yards ahead of me going for it when he slipped, and the ball bounced right up into my hands.

You couldn't have scripted it any better for a nervous youngster in his first big championship game. That bounce of the ball was the bit of luck I needed to settle me.

Later on in that half Alan Cronin got past Séamus and was coming down the line when I met him with a shoulder and got him over the line.

In the Munster final later that year Séamus repaid the favour when Stephen Kelly got past me down the sideline: another lesson for me, because even though it was a man-on-man game, there was always the chance of a dig-out from a team-mate, and the chance you'd have to give them a dig-out in turn.

From early on I'd have been hard on myself anyway, but when you've only one job – to keep your man scoreless – there can be an obvious drawback. What happens when he *does* get a score?

We beat Cork by eight points on the day and after the game, walking down into Killarney town and being approached by people shaking my hand was almost surreal. The place was jam-packed with over 40,000 supporters; our neighbours from Cork always loved to travel to Killarney and it made for a carnival atmosphere in the town – GAA at its best.

But we were back training soon enough. Limerick were next up in the Munster final. They were a serious, serious team around that time, with plenty of experience, and with Liam Kearns and Donie Buckley involved, they'd be well prepared. Donie was one of the best coaches around and would bring my game to a whole new level when he got involved with Kerry in the years after; he was the best defensive coach I had during my career.

On the Thursday after the Cork game Jack came over to me and said, 'Mahony, we're thinking of putting you on Stephen Kelly.'

The great thing about Jack's approach was that he didn't leave it at that. He said all I had to do was stick with Kelly because every time he got the ball he was going to run with it, and he told me not to pay attention to anything else that was happening on the field.

'You'll have the legs for him,' said Jack.

The year before, I'd seen Kelly make hay against Kerry and I'd said to myself, *I could mark him*, and now I was getting the chance to do just that.

We had a ferocious battle with them in the Munster final, the first day above in Limerick. They were in our faces from the first minute – not that I had anything against that, I was well able to mind myself, but it was another learning curve for me. They were savagely competitive, which was only to be expected, but there's a world of difference between hearing the term 'savagely competitive' and dealing with it in the flesh.

At one stage early on Stephen got a ball on the stand side around his own 45 and took off like a rocket.

Here we go, I thought.

I stayed with him as he went up the line – the crowd rising to him as he went – but I managed to turn him inside. The second time he went I stayed with him as well, but it was a fair test.

Still, I was able for it. The hard training was paying off. Even before I went in with Kerry, people would have suggested I was short a yard of pace, yet here I was keeping up with one of the fastest players in the game.

The next time he got inside me, but as I mentioned earlier, Séamus got back to put him over the end line. Stephen was relentless. After three runs another player might have taken a break, but he was just getting started.

The next time, though, I got a hand in and flicked the ball away from him, but while I was shielding the ball out over the line he hit me a belt of a shoulder and turned me upside down.

I got up and hit him a dig in the ribs and he went down. I was thinking, *Oh God, what have I done here?* There was a roar from the crowd nearby and I was trying to spot where the referee was when I realised most people were watching a Jack Russell dog which had run onto the pitch at the other end of the stadium. Another stroke of luck.

The obvious question is where my career would have gone if I'd been sent off there and then, particularly a sending-off I couldn't have argued with. Marc Ó Sé was coming back from club duty, Séamus was still injured, so if I'd been sent off and suspended they'd have slotted in for future games – if the team could even win a game like that with 14 men. Looking back, it was madness.

At the time I can't remember who sorted the dog out at the other end of the ground – maybe the referee sent him off instead of me – but Stephen got back up off the ground, and the whole thing blew over because there was so much going on elsewhere.

That was the day Limerick had a couple of 45s late on that would have won the game for them, but Darragh Ó Sé pulled them down from over the crossbar. Draw.

Jack wasn't too happy with what I'd done. I got a bit of a cuffing over it, which was no harm: I might have been only a young lad but I couldn't be taking the law into my own hands. And I took the lesson on board, that I couldn't be the reason Kerry lost a game because of something like that.

There was plenty of talk about the incident after the game, but it was a time when video analysis on *The*

Sunday Game wasn't as sophisticated, and there was more of a sense that if the referee didn't put it in his report, then it was over and done with.

We met the Thursday night before the replay and Jack said I'd be on Stephen again. Grand.

The replay took place in a packed Fitzgerald stadium. Heaving. Fantastic atmosphere.

When we lined out, though, Stephen went into the corner, while I was left outside on the wing on Stephen Lavin. Tom O'Sullivan picked Kelly up instead.

The ball was thrown in and driven into Kelly ... and bang! He hammered it into the roof of the net. Then he trotted out to me and hit me a belt of a shoulder. Game on.

We came back and beat them but myself and Stephen had a fantastic tussle. What I loved about the guy was his attitude. As every young player should realise, sometimes in games it may not happen for you, but you have to persist. Stephen didn't know the meaning of giving up, hence when people ask me about my toughest opponent he ranks up there with the best.

Winning that game gave me huge confidence. To start and finish it, along with the drawn game before that, instilled a belief in me that I could survive at that level. Séamus got injured, so that had opened the door for me, but still – I'd got over the line.

Even the fact that Stephen got that early goal ... I could have lost concentration and got distracted in the game, thinking I should have been picking him up when he scored it, but I didn't.

That showed me I could focus in a big game, focus on what I had to do.

Getting a first Munster medal was a huge boost. I couldn't say I'd spent every night since the age of eight praying to play in a Munster final for Kerry, but when I got there I was determined to win it.

The win got us an August date with Dublin in the All-Ireland quarter-finals.

Croke Park. The Dubs. The Golden Years. Micko, Heffo. The back story to every Kerry–Dublin game since then, but at that stage it was new to me. A bit of hype was beginning to build around the game, which again was novel for yours truly, whose last visit there had been as a sub on the Kerry minors.

I remember picking out Senan Connell as a direct runner, someone who'd travel all day long – even then there was a lot of discussion about just how fit the Dublin players were – and in the game itself I started off on him. He started running at the beginning of the game. And never stopped.

I struggled to catch my breath because, despite what I'd experienced against Cork and Limerick in the Munster championship, this was a different level altogether.

I almost got a break when we went down low for a ball and clashed heads. Almost. He cut his head and went off to get that stitched up, so Mossy Quinn came on to replace him.

As he was coming on, Tommy Lyons, the Dublin boss, was roaring at him to keep running, and Mossy, in fairness, took the message on board – he started running over and back, over and back, over and back, across the field from sideline to sideline. It's interesting to look back on that now because I'd say I was within a couple of seconds of giving up because of the physical intensity of it. I felt like I couldn't keep going at all, that I wasn't up to the challenge of it.

The encouragement to keep going came from an unlikely source, or couple of sources. On one of those cross-field runs tracking Mossy I caught sight of Tom O'Sullivan and Mike McCarthy inside me, and each of them was as pale as I was.

Hang on, I thought, *it's not just me who's suffering here.*

That wasn't much consolation when Senan came back on, because he just took off like a hare again. I'd never experienced anything like that, the constant movement – these fellas weren't just darting here and there, but making 70-, 80-, 90-metre runs. Over and over again.

It was one of the sharpest examples of the difference between championship level and everything else: in the championship everything happens at top speed, and it doesn't let up.

Years of surviving training – of telling myself to hang on in there and get through it – were a help to me, but I also had a job to do. It wouldn't be enough to say to myself at full-time that I survived. But as the game wore on I got into it. I won a couple of balls, even though at that stage of my senior career I was very conservative – I minded the house and tended to stay inside my man rather than trying to win the ball coming in.

Senan kicked two frees but hadn't scored from play, and Tom and Mike Mac were really squeezing their men, but even so we weren't pulling away until Darragh pumped a high ball in to Dara Ó Cinnéide and he got a goal. That gave us breathing space and took the wind out of their sails: we pushed on to win by seven points.

Afterwards I put it down as another milestone. I'd played three games and kept my man scoreless, and I wanted to continue that run. Páidí Ó Sé was in charge of Westmeath on the other side of the draw and the stars seemed to be aligning for a Kerry versus Páidí reunion – until Derry turned them over to meet us in the semi-final.

They had some tasty players in the likes of Paddy Bradley, Conleth Gilligan and Enda Muldoon, who got an early goal against us. They had a good game plan, feeding Bradley and Muldoon, while we were playing route one ourselves, getting the ball into our full-forward line.

With Mike Frank Russell, Dara Ó Cinnéide and Colm Cooper up there it was a matter of getting them the ball as quickly as we could, but we also had Declan O'Sullivan giving us a different dimension further out the field, carrying the ball and play-making.

Darragh came off injured and Séamus Moynihan didn't start because he had a knock, so if you were a Derry player you'd probably fancy your chances at that point given who was missing – two of our marquee players.

But what I remember is feeling there was an extra onus on the rest of us to stand up because they were gone. Also, at the time there was a narrative that the Kerry backs would be vulnerable if you got at them one-on-one (as though there were ever backs who wouldn't feel vulnerable if you got at them one-on-one).

We were conscious of standing up to that, of making a statement.

Derry didn't score for 30 minutes of the second half.

My man was replaced in the game, and here my experience against Dublin helped me: I knew from that game that whoever came in was going to be hungry and run non-stop, and when it happened I was prepared for it. Another lesson.

At the final whistle we were six points up and looking forward to an All-Ireland final against Mayo.

My thinking after the semi-final wasn't centred on enjoying the experience of the build-up, soaking up the atmosphere. It was more along the lines of *Have I enough done to start?*

Was that selfish? But Séamus was coming back, and Marc had done well against Derry. Seven players into six positions wouldn't go; I hadn't played in an All-Ireland final yet, and the rest of them had. But I enjoyed the run-in to the final despite that.

On the Tuesday night Sean Hussey from Tralee came in to sort us out for the suits, so getting the inside leg measured up was a milestone.

There was a media day, which was another eye-opener for me. I remember there was a piece describing me as the bedrock from Rathmore, and I thought that was great.

We'd have been warned not to talk too much about the game, but if I was asked a question I'd answer away. Now, the answer mightn't have been what the questioner wanted, because I usually just talked about how much Tom and Mike Mac had helped me all year rather than straying into anything remotely controversial. Or interesting.

The open day for the supporters made it more real. It was a glimpse of what Kerry football means, when you see former greats bring their own kids in for photographs and autographs.

I was still working for Dawn Dairies, so everywhere the van went I had people talking to me about the game, but I took the Friday off work to avoid that – which was probably the worst thing I could have done, because instead of being distracted, I just spent the day thinking about the game.

Jack would have rung me that week to feel me out, and after a bit of chit-chat he told me I'd start at corner-back, probably picking up Brian Maloney; Tom would start on Conor Mortimer, Éamonn would mark Ciarán McDonald, Tomás and Marc on the wings and Mike at number 3. Séamus was still coming back from injury and was on the bench.

That was great news, but as soon as it sank in the nerves started to bite. The hype was building about Mayo and the famine (they hadn't won an All-Ireland since 1951), and their forwards were exceptional, but what stood to me was the fact that I hadn't played in an All-Ireland final. Nervous as I was, those nerves didn't have a basis in reality for me yet.

In short, I didn't know what was ahead of me.

The trip up was a story in itself: playing cards with the Ó Sé brothers is always a losing proposition, and by the time the train passed Portlaoise there was a considerable transfer of wealth to west Kerry. (Which serves more of a purpose than you'd think. It's a good distraction for a long day's travelling, even if your wallet would be lighter by the time you landed into Heuston.)

That night in the hotel in Dublin there would be a team meeting. Jack would ask a few of the lads to speak. Séamus and Dara Ó Cinnéide were fantastic speakers in that kind of environment. They were fellas who could leave you with tears in your eyes, talking about what the jersey meant to them and to the people at home.

That can be a bit of a realisation for new players – you're so focused for the first few months on training properly and getting yourself right for matches, dealing with the pressure of your first full season on the team, that you don't take a step back and see what it means to represent Kerry.

These were lads who had won All-Irelands, who had lost All-Irelands, and they were sharing their experiences. It was emotional, even though I spent most of the time thinking, *Please don't ask me to speak.*

Those meetings were a huge help. People might think that firing fellas up on the Saturday night isn't much help for a game that's not on until the following afternoon, but by that Saturday evening, even though you're well focused on the job you have the following day, someone might make a point to get you to focus on something different about your game.

You might have every angle covered, but someone may say, 'Don't drop the head if something happens early on: you've 65 minutes to put it right.'

A few of the lads got a rub, but as a new player I didn't feel it was my place to hop up on the table, that that was something for the experienced lads, to relax them. Maybe I should have had a rub, though, because I didn't sleep well at all, and neither did Paul Galvin, who roomed with me.

Tossing and turning. When I got up the following morning it was the usual trick – I seemed to fall into a deep, deep sleep about five minutes before the alarm clock went off.

On the way down to the breakfast we met Ger O'Keeffe, who was a selector, and who'd be bright as a button whether he slept for an hour or 10 hours the night before.

'How are ye, lads?'

'Ger, I didn't sleep a wink last night,' I said.

Quick as a flash he came back: 'Don't mind that, Maurice Fitzgerald didn't sleep a wink the night before the 1997 All-Ireland final and he went out and kicked 9 points.'

Myself and Paul burst out laughing. He came out with it so quickly he couldn't have made it up on the spot, but it put us at ease.

After breakfast we had a walk and Mass. There were a few cards at reception for me from people, which was a nice touch.

Then up to get dressed. New tracksuit. New polo top taken out of the plastic wrapper. The build-up to the minor game on the television in the room; the sound of the Irish-language commentary telling you that it's coming.

And then I started to feel the butterflies. I had the bag packed with three hours to spare but my mind was racing with all the possibilities and permutations. If this happens. If that happens. This scenario. That one.

Brian Maloney was my sole focus, and marking him, but going outside to the bus it hit home. This is real. This final is going to happen, and soon.

I sat in the front with Tom O'Sullivan – and would spend 10 years in the front seat afterwards – and that was just the tonic I needed for those games. Tom would nearly read that morning's paper to see what they were writing about him.

As the bus rolled on and the stadium got closer, there were more and more people decked head to toe in their county colours, and by the time we were approaching Jones's Road it was all green and red or green and gold.

Then the bus turned through the big gates and we were there. Croke Park.

6

First Final

Recovering from an Early Setback

The little things surprise you on All-Ireland final day – for example, the programme. From club games you'd be used to a sheet of paper with the names on it – a few of them crossed out with biro and replacements scribbled in – but in Croke Park that day there was a thick magazine, a full picture of every player and details of their likes and dislikes. (I kept the flag flying for tradition by naming steak as my favourite food, though Pink as my favourite singer doesn't sound like me.)

Seeing the name of the club struck a chord with me, and I started to think about that – *So many from Rathmore are here to support myself and Tom; it's a huge day for the club.* The weather was balmy, so I decided to get a breath of fresh air, and I went out to see a bit of the minor game. Then we togged out and Jack spoke. Then Dara Ó Cinnéide spoke. He was a phenomenal captain and gave a great speech: all relevant facts, what we were doing and what we were about.

The game plan was simple. Johnny Crowley had come in for Mike Frank and Jack said we were going to test out the Mayo full-back line and see what they were made of.

'Kick it in to Johnny,' said Jack. 'That's what he's in there for.'

That was great news to a back, because it meant route one was an option if you were under pressure. (In the game itself I put two skyscrapers in on top of him; in the modern game I'd have been whipped off before the second one even landed, but that was our approach in 2004.)

Night after night in training we saw Johnny winning balls that were 90/10 against him through raw power, he was that strong.

What many people didn't pick up on, though, was Éamonn Fitzmaurice's ability to deliver good ball: he was a beautiful kicker of the ball and delivered great missiles into Johnny under instructions from Jack, who said to persist with the tactic even if the first couple of deliveries didn't work out.

There was a backing track to Dara and Jack's speeches: the noise of the crowd was rumbling and growing all the time as throw-in got closer.

People might expect to hear that players were nauseous with the nerves, but the atmosphere was calm. I took my cue from Tom, whose coolness rubbed off on me to some extent.

Lining out alongside himself and Mike Mac was calming enough, though, because I knew they were good enough to bail me out if I got in trouble.

All things considered I was pretty relaxed and content – until I was reminded about the formalities: meeting the president, marching behind the Artane Boys Band and parading around the pitch pre-throw-in.

I was thinking, *Should I look up into the crowd to see if I recognise anyone, or should I stare at the man marching in front of me?*

Then it was out into the light.

The noise is deafening, and to experience that noise coming at you, it's almost a physical blow.

I definitely lost myself for a minute or two. I remember jumping into the air just to release some of the adrenaline.

Pat Flanagan, the strength and conditioning coach, told me to fall in for the warm-up, and that settled me. I remember thinking players were jumping higher and running harder in the warm-up than they usually did, that everything was happening at a faster pace.

Then the teams were announced over the PA, and I heard my own name being called out. There was nothing like hearing the support when that happened.

I did what I'd done for years, picking out my man as he warmed up at the other end. I paid close attention to Brian Maloney's kicking style and how he ran. And then the subs were called ashore.

Lining up to meet the president, you'd almost think we were going to have a long conversation, but it was just a handshake, and gone.

I'd never experienced anything like the parade. The noise, the colour, the emotion flowing down out of the stands and the terraces. Going past Hill 16, packed to the rafters with Mayo supporters, it was like a physical thing, the wall of noise coming out of it. That ramps up the nerves to a fairly high pitch. When we finally went into the huddle, the anthem struck up. The nerves in the stomach reached fever pitch then. In a minute the game would be on. The All-Ireland final.

I was down at the Hill 16 end and Alan Dillon ran in to mark me, the number 12 jersey on his back. Brian Maloney was out in the half-forward line.

I had a flashback to the Munster final replay, when Stephen Kelly went in to the full-forward line: should I stay or go out and pick up the man I was assigned? But then the ball was thrown in, so I said I'd stay with Dillon unless I was told otherwise.

After a couple of minutes Trevor Mortimer came up the Cusack stand side of the field and put the ball in diagonally. Tom went for it alongside Conor Mortimer, and got in front of Conor, but slipped; Mortimer didn't realise the ball was coming to him and it bounced over his head. I came out for it but I slipped too (just a result of playing on unfamiliar ground), and the ball landed in Alan Dillon's lap.

I got up and tried to get back, and so did Tom: I was looking in at Diarmuid Murphy in goal and thinking of the great saves he'd made all year, but Dillon went around him and hit the back of the net.

Hill 16 exploded.

I was thinking to myself, *How do I come back from this?*

In the previous games nobody had scored from play off me, and here I was leaking a goal in the first couple of minutes of an All-Ireland final.

It's a lonely patch of grass when that happens. There's no sports psychologist there to help you through it. For me it was the worst nightmare I could imagine, conceding a goal and watching it unfold almost in slow motion. All the training. All the preparation. All the things I hung my confidence on. All for nothing when the ball was thrown in.

Almost from the kick-out Ciarán McDonald put a ball over the bar with the outside of his boot: 55 metres out, no problem.

Alan Dillon moved out after the goal and Brian Maloney came in to the corner. I refocused on him, told myself to get tight, but the goal really affected me.

I was shaken by it, naturally enough. Every time the ball came near my corner there seemed – to me, anyway – to be a huge amount of noise from the Mayo support. I was nervous, no two ways about it: in the All-Ireland semi-final, when I was top of my game, I was going out to field balls cleanly, but after the goal I was trying to break it away. Little things like that can give away a player's state of mind in a game.

Dillon had a free outfield and Maloney made a dart for it; I had him covered but he took the ball and swung it over the black spot.

I was on the hook for 1–1 already after just a few minutes: I even looked up at the clock to see how much time had gone, which you're not encouraged to do at any point in a game, but that's how desperate I was by then.

In fact I was beginning to look over to the sideline to see who they were warming up. My thoughts were negative: *You're not involved in the game.*

Later, when I watched the game back, I saw how I'd slipped, how my feet had gone, but there was another lesson to be learned from that video clip.

Tom had slipped as well but his first instinct was to get up and burst himself trying to get back. I was still pulling myself up, but he was getting back because there was always a chance – that Diarmuid would pull off the save or that Dillon would hit the post or bar.

That was experience at work. Later in my career I could have told myself about the goal – that it wasn't my fault. And I could have talked myself through Brian Maloney's point – that he'd swung a boot without even looking at the goal and it happened to sail over. But that comes with experience.

The ironic thing is that I'd be the first person now to say to a young player, 'If your man hits a point from 40 metres, then that's major credit to him, forget it and move on,' but I couldn't convince myself of that in the middle of a game in 2004.

I didn't know how to get out of that zone, but then I caught a break. The ball came in long and Maloney went for it, but it carried over his head and I caught it.

After that he started drifting out the field, and when I followed him I got on more ball. I put a long one in to Johnny which was 60/40 against him, but he won it and pointed. Another positive.

Looking back, I give huge credit to Jack and the selectors. It would have been easy to cut their losses after 10 minutes and say, 'This is a young player in his first All-Ireland, we'll take him off,' but they backed me.

If I had been in their shoes I might have made that switch: Séamus Moynihan was waiting in the wings, not a bad option to bring in and shore up your defence.

It was a lesson I took with me. The first ball was a disaster for me, and the second wasn't much better, but there's always a third ball, and a fourth ball. It was a tough arena to learn that lesson in, with 80,000 people roaring at me. Maybe that was the reason the lesson stayed with me.

At half-time we were 1–12 to 1–4 ahead, so after the glitches in the first 10 minutes we were going well.

Management were very diplomatic. They said I was getting into the game and they stressed that the goal hadn't been my fault.

'That can happen to anyone,' they said, and that changed my mind. Maybe they were right, I thought, maybe it wasn't my fault. It was easy to dent my confidence but Jack knew how to manage me and knew what I needed to hear.

We were eight points up but while Jack and the selectors were keen to point out that a goal would bring Mayo back into the game, we were well in control.

Gooch was un-markable up front. When he got his goal after a fetch and a jink it was poetry in motion, and the axis he formed with Dara and Johnny was lethal.

Another player who was outstanding that day was William Kirby in the middle of the field. He hit three points from play and showed that there wasn't a need to be collecting man of the match awards to get the respect of your peers – and few players had the respect of their peers like William. He was vital that day, with his unusual kicking style.

Conor Mortimer had a goal chance that he put over the bar late on – he had more time than he realised, and a goal would have made it a four-point game. By the time Mickey Conroy came on and got a goal for Mayo, we were well ahead.

In the last seven or eight minutes the thought came into my head: *There's a possibility here that I'll win an All-Ireland medal.*

The Mayo supporters were starting to leave – you could see the lines of people going up the walkways out of the stand – and it was clear we were going to win.

I remember feeling as though a weight was being lifted off my shoulders, a feeling of *I got here*. The challenge at the start of the year had been all about getting on the panel, and before the end of the All-Ireland final I remember thinking about the league and getting myself onto the team for the championship ... I got emotional, because I was thinking about where I'd come from and the battle to get here, which in hindsight I loved.

Then the final whistle went. That was a time when crowds could still come onto the field in Croke Park at the end of a game. My brother was out to me, tears in his eyes, people from Rathmore hugging me, Tom leaning in and saying, 'Your first All-Ireland' ... it's raw emotion. As I was trying to get up to see the Hogan stand, I saw people crying and laughing, a whole range of emotions showing what an All-Ireland means.

That hadn't sunk in for me – maybe because I was so focused on playing all that year – but it made an impression on me that particular day.

One of my main memories was meeting up with Séamus Moynihan and Darragh Ó Sé out on the field and being hugged by them, two gods of the game.

Another was walking up the steps of the Hogan stand. It's funny to read or hear that so often, players talking about the experience of going up the steps when they win an All-Ireland.

But when I did it myself, and looked down on the cordon of security people holding the supporters back, I understood why they talked about it. It was like nothing you could imagine.

Dara made his speech in Irish and lifted the Sam Maguire. Séamus was next to me and squeezed me with the emotion of it, and the reaction of thousands of people on the pitch mirrored that feeling.

I got up to the top of the steps and shook hands with everyone who was there because all I wanted was to get my hands on the Sam Maguire and lift it. When I did, it felt amazing. The battle was worth it.

As an experience it was everything I could have imagined – and more.

Immediately afterwards, inside in the dressing room, you're wondering what's next. For me it was family. I got a message that my family were outside, so I went out and met them, and that was a moment to cherish. The game itself had gone by in a flash – with the exception of those opening minutes – but having that time with them was a special experience.

The dressing room was wild with victory. A sing-song started, water was being sprayed around, Sean Walsh the chairman came in wearing his good suit – a great character – and the Ó Sés started blackguarding him with more water. It's euphoria, pure and simple. Nobody wants the feeling to end. Kick off the boots. Savour it.

We pulled on the tracksuits to head to the players' lounge, and all the families of the players were there.

The media were outside, but I was pretty sure they'd be more interested in Gooch or Kirby, who'd been outstanding in the game. I was also conscious that I'd conceded that goal early on, which was something I had no interest in reliving in an interview.

I relived it with Johnny Culloty, another of Jack's selectors, who had a great manner. He pointed out that those things happen in big games, that I'd come back from it. And that I'd done well, keeping my man scoreless after.

There was a fair contrast between the bus journey in that morning and heading back to the hotel afterwards. There weren't many Mayo supporters, and the Kerry crowd applauded and cheered us every time they saw the bus.

Back at the hotel I walked in behind Dara, who had the Sam Maguire in his hands, and people lined his route into the hotel and through the lobby: an unbelievable reception.

I changed into the suit. I wasn't a suit man really, so my dad made up the knot in the tie for me on the Friday. It served me well that evening.

It's a special night. Everyone's family is there, *The Sunday Game* comes on and in my mind I was flicking back to being a kid watching the show at home.

Of course, when the match itself came on I didn't enjoy the first few minutes – Tom enjoyed reminding me of it at the table – but it settled down. Gooch took home the man of the match award, which was well deserved.

Later on in the evening we all dropped in to the live event in the hotel, which was jammed with Kerry supporters who'd had a long, enjoyable day.

The players were introduced to the supporters onstage by the great Niall 'Botty' O'Callaghan, who would go on to be a great friend of mine and play a huge part in my career when he became involved with the Kerry backroom team.

By the time Tom and I were introduced, everyone from Rathmore had come to the front of the stage, and they were right in front of us.

That was special, and the whole place was rocking. There were Kerry people in the hotel who were living all over the world but who'd made the effort to come back for the game. It was a day – and a night – to remember.

7

'Has This Really Happened?'

Homecoming

The morning after an All-Ireland final you come downstairs to the lobby of the team hotel and one of the first things you see is the media, waiting for players.

That's something that would get you to straighten yourself up fairly fast, whether you'd been in bed for the whole night or half an hour.

Bringing the Sam Maguire out to Crumlin children's hospital on the Monday morning has become a huge part of the post-All-Ireland celebration, and it's a fantastic experience, particularly for me in later years as a member of An Garda Síochána. There's an escort out there, and once you land in with the cup you can see the lift it gives the kids and their parents alike.

It gives a player perspective, too, about their own privileged position. You've played in an All-Ireland final not 24 hours earlier and were probably never fitter in your life; you've achieved a lifetime goal by winning – but seeing what people are facing out in the hospital in Crumlin puts it all in context.

Back at the hotel it's a matter of cramming the gear bag with all the bits that were carefully ironed and laid out beautifully a couple of days before: for the return trip there's just a bulge of clothes in the bag.

I didn't have my Kerry jersey for the gear bag: I'd swapped it, and when people asked me about it I always said it meant more to me to be standing beside Séamus Moynihan and Éamonn Fitzmaurice at the steps of the Hogan stand than having a jersey on my back. (A couple of people had spotted me there and asked me later about everything I was taking in. In truth I didn't know what to even look at by that stage, but later in my career I made sure to savour everything at moments like that.)

Filing onto the bus for the train home was actually a buzz for me because I could remember chatting to Tom about 2000, when he and Declan O'Keeffe were on the Kerry team that won the All-Ireland. He had described how sweet that was, bringing the cup to Rathmore on the train, and I have to admit it was on my mind even as the train pulled out of Heuston station.

It's a great journey. Fellas are relaxed, having a couple of beers – some fellas are very relaxed indeed, given they mightn't have gone to bed the night before – and for me every mile was bringing me closer to Rathmore, my home club, my home.

Thurles. Charleville. Banteer. Millstreet. For years going up and down on the train those names meant nothing, but on that journey they were the countdown to home.

Before we got to Rathmore I popped into the bathroom to straighten up the tie and fix the hair, and then we were there.

From the very start of the platform the place was thronged with people, waving flags. I get emotional even thinking about it now because I appreciate what it means. Not every player on the panel has the train stopping at their home place, and when the cup starts doing the rounds around the county in the weeks that follow there are always a couple of lads who can't make a particular stop.

But the whole travelling party was together in Rathmore. The entire team. We were right on the Cork–Kerry border with the cup and everyone was together: it was magic.

The train came to a stop and the cup was brought down to myself and Tom. We could hear Tina Turner's 'Simply the Best' blaring outside.

When we got off the train we got a great reception, and what made it really special was the fact that our families were allowed in to greet us near the gate on the platform – family, nieces and nephews, all there to embrace us. It was a great touch because it made a big event feel very intimate.

My own family had left Dublin for home that morning and it was the first chance I had to really talk to them. They were in the hotel for the banquet but you can't really talk to people properly there because of the crowds milling around.

A lot of those people would have put down an entire year following the team around. From league games, even, you'd recognise the odd face, people you'd get to know over the various Januaries and Februaries supporting the team. If you saw those people the night of the All-Ireland banquet you'd be sure to have a chat and thank them.

But on the platform in Rathmore I got to have a few minutes to chat with the family and to get a few pictures taken. We were all led out then, the whole team, and put up on the back of a lorry, and we could get a proper look at the crowd: thousands of people, the entire population of Rathmore, and more people besides.

You'd be trying hard not to cry, in all honesty. The adrenaline has seeped away and you're running on fumes after a long night, so by the time we got to Rathmore we were flagging a bit.

Still, when the team was introduced you knew who the stars were – the roar for Gooch would be heard in Timbuktu, for instance – but it was also noticeable that the personalities of the players emerged, the characters we knew from all those training sessions and games.

The only thing that was really occupying my mind was what I'd say to the crowd. Public speaking wouldn't be something I'd be keen on at the best of times, so I'd settled on a plan with Tom as to what we'd do.

'I'll cover this, and you cover that.'

'Sound.'

And of course when it came to taking the microphone, Tom went first and covered this and covered that and everything else besides.

Then he handed me the mic: 'There you go, Mahony.'

I did my best: I tried to remember people who'd passed away, everyone who'd helped us along, but of course it hardly mattered what I was saying. The crowd was in such good humour that they'd have cheered me anyway.

Looking back, I realise that a lot of the lads in the crowd that night would go on to become team-mates of mine – with Rathmore and Kerry – while other snapshots stuck with me too, including Donal Murphy and the late Frank Buckley calling out the players' names and that roar when they were introduced.

I'd never have dreamed of playing with Kerry, but waving the Sam Maguire at the crowd in Rathmore was fulfilling something that thousands upon thousands of people did dream of. I was very conscious of that.

We left eventually and rolled on to Tralee, where there were 25,000 people waiting for us. Killarney the same, a carnival atmosphere in the whole town, and I was thinking, *Did anyone go to work today at all in the county?*

It began to sink in then. This is Kerry football, and this is what it means to people. The months of hard training, everything that's given up for the cause, that's what it all culminates in.

Being an inter-county player is a selfish commitment. Some players won't say so, but it's true. The hours that are put in, the sacrifices, they're all for a night like that, when everyone can glory in it.

If I put sacrifices in the context of my entire career, start to finish, the one thing I'd say is this: it's a player's choice.

From the outside people might say, 'They're making some sacrifices,' but when you're inside the bubble it's not a sacrifice but a choice. You're an elite athlete, in there with 30 or 35 other fellas.

What you're doing all the time is evaluating what you can do. Can I go for a walk? Will I go for a jog up the mountain?

The question, then, is whether those are choices or sacrifices. When I fell out of love with the game between

2009 and '10, those were sacrifices because my mind was telling me they were.

But in the last few seasons of my career I had a totally different perspective: I felt it was a gift to still be involved with Kerry, and it was rewarding to be going through that tough training, those hard sessions. When I was written off in 2009 I took it badly; when I was written off in 2013 I was motivated to work harder. I loved the challenge.

Part of that is trying to improve yourself by a couple of per cent. If you take a nap, if you make a small change to your diet – some people might see that as a sacrifice, but someone who's serious about winning an All-Ireland medal sees it as another little improvement to move a little closer to the ultimate goal.

The reality is that the real sacrifices are the ones your family makes. They're the people who don't see you because of training or have to organise things around you and your timetable. Those are real sacrifices.

Because Dara Ó Cinnéide was captain, we ended up in west Kerry – a huge marquee in the village of An Bóthar, and yours truly trying to squeeze out the *cúpla focail* with the native speakers.

It's a great week. You're never tired because the adrenaline kicks in when you see the reaction people have to the cup, but for all that I was happy enough to head back home on the Tuesday.

Leaving Killarney, once I hit Barraduff on the way out the pictures along the roadside appeared. By that I mean pictures of myself and Tom, which was surreal.

Coming through Rathmore to the home place, there must have been 10 or 15 pictures of myself and Tom with good luck messages on them, as well as bunting and flags. I'd have been staying away from all of that in the build-up, but I took it all in afterwards.

Pulling in at home I saw the colours they'd put up all over the house, the green and gold, and I really knew it was a big deal when I saw all the papers folded on top of the kitchen table.

My dad was cutting out pictures to get his scrapbook going, while my mom was telling me where the good articles were.

We had a cup of tea and a chat, with my phone hopping all the time – 'The cup is going here today, then it's going here' – while Mom was suggesting maybe a night at home wouldn't be any harm and when was I going back to work?

Looking out for me. As always.

I was keen to get back with the club, even though it was a long season with Kerry. Part of it was wanting to help out the club, but part of it was trying to get back to normality as well. I enjoyed the celebrations hugely, but I knew that wasn't real life either.

But when I fell back in with Rathmore I was fatigued.

The long season was beginning to catch up with me and the body was wearing down a bit.

Time isn't long moving on, either. Soon enough we were in October. I was about to start a new job, as an official member of An Garda Síochána (having completed my training over the summer). And the O'Donoghue cup – also known as the east Kerry divisional championship – was on the horizon, and the dynamic is different with the club when you're a Kerry player. Every player in every other club is out to take you down.

I fell back in as a centre-back with Rathmore, and it was in my mind to play as a traditional centre-back: a man-marker.

My logic was simple. If I didn't blot my man out, people would be reading all over Kerry in the match reports that such-and-such got three points, or four points, from play off Aidan O'Mahony.

I was determined that that wasn't going to happen. Looking into 2005 I felt there was still some uncertainty surrounding the make-up of the team. Séamus Moynihan had been injured for a lot of 2004, Darragh Ó Sé the same, but both of them would come back into the team, no question about that.

Looking around, I saw promising youngsters like Kieran Donaghy, Pádraig Reidy and Darran O'Sullivan coming into contention, so I knew I had to cement my position.

It was a time when there really was an off-season: you didn't have a strength and conditioning coach getting in touch with a training programme or checking up on whether you were in the club gym. Very few clubs had gyms, to begin with.

There were club games every weekend anyway to keep us going, but that winter we also had our night with the cup in Rathmore.

That's a special occasion. It's a community function as much as anything, because the cup is carried to the community centre and the kids get their photo taken with it, and then there are a few drinks as it's brought around the pubs of the village.

That's where the balancing act comes in too, because the cup obviously goes to the club of every player on the panel, and when it does it's accompanied by a few other players as well. But if you went to every one of those you'd be in a cruel way, because each event is a huge night for that club. And it's non-stop right up to December, when there are various socials and a team photo is taken out at Muckross House.

It was nearly 2005 when we got our All-Ireland medals. Having it in my hand made it all real, and walking down to the table I was sitting at in the Gleneagle hotel in Killarney, handing it over to my parents and seeing their reaction as they looked at it – there was a sense of writing it into the history books.

I'd often say that playing football isn't about winning medals. They end up in a biscuit tin or a drawer somewhere, and it's the memories of the games and battles that stay with you. But in the moment, my name being called out at that function organised by the Kerry county board, walking up to have the medal handed to me and getting a picture taken ... that was special, the medal and the memory.

Even that evening, though, Jack would have mentioned the coming year, the need to freshen up the panel. Waking up the morning after the function I realised the amount of work ahead of me.

In 2004 I'd been there but my position wasn't set in stone, I felt. Pat Flanagan handed out a training programme. For 2005 I'd have to ramp up my preparations to another level.

When you start any season it's the last thing on your mind – the Monday morning after winning an All-Ireland final. And certainly not as a first-time winner.

The thousands of Kerry people who'd gone up for the match had now headed back home to welcome the victorious team, and I was standing in Heuston station boarding the train with their heroes, pinching myself: *Has this really happened?*

The fairytale played out: Rathmore, my home club, the club that nurtured me from a young age, the reason I graced Croke Park the previous day, was the first stop where Sam Maguire would be welcomed back to the Kingdom.

The train pulled up. There was music blaring, bonfires blazing for miles to see, thousands of people chanting my name. I walked out to the podium and the noise of the crowd vibrated through my body. It was absolute euphoria. A memory for a lifetime.

8

'He's Short a Yard of Pace'

2005 and Building My Fitness

Jack was as good as his word when it came to fresh-ening things up. Nothing keeps a panel of players on their toes like new faces walking in through the dressing-room door, and when you factor in that Séamus and Darragh were coming back from injury – lads who weren't going to be content just riding the bench – the competition was heating up.

I wanted a jersey, simple as that. One thing that stood to me was management's approach to selection at that time – it was an era when the championship team was played almost man for man in league games, so if you were the man in possession of the jersey you had a decent chance of holding onto it. In the earlier years I'd seen how that worked from the other side, when I was trying to break in, and how tough it was when you were trying to make a name for yourself.

Training-wise 2004 had been good for me. Pat Flanagan's sessions were tailored for us, so you had heavy training weeks, which were three tough days in the gym and three tough running days on the pitch. Then there'd be a de-load week, which was all football.

But we knew in 2005 that the previous year's approach wasn't going to get us over the line. Tyrone hadn't gone away, Cork were coming back strong after we'd beaten them well in 2004, and other teams were getting themselves organised.

Part of the approach in 2005 would have been driven by Pat Flanagan thinking, *Last year most of the players bought into the gym work, but I'll need the whole panel doing it this year and going to another level.*

So we were put into pods going to the gym in the Gleneagle hotel in Killarney and other places close to players, driving each other on. And the likes of Séamus and Darragh were driving lads as much as anybody on the pitch because they knew their own careers were coming to an end and they wanted more All-Ireland medals.

Pat was a fantastic strength and conditioning coach – he was years ahead of his time – and he designed great programmes for us, and we wouldn't stray from them.

We realised it was becoming more and more important to incorporate the gym into our preparation, and the more time I spent in the gym, the more I got out of it. Not just benefits in terms of playing, but I began to realise how much I enjoyed it as an experience in itself.

I loved the gym from the very start. Everyone finds something in life they like doing, and for me at that point it was the gym, definitely.

Looking back, I was an easy athlete to train. I was always on time and did everything to a T: the discipline of training came very naturally to me, which might relate back to my childhood. From working on the farm you get into a routine of what you do on a daily basis, and time is the biggest discipline when getting work done.

I learned to get through the work when I had to do it, rather than putting it off, and I took the same approach to the gym.

Now, there were perks involved with the gym. We had a dip in the pool afterwards or sat in the sauna. It wasn't all hard work.

But behind it all I knew I needed the gym work. I was still too light. I'd got away with that in 2004, and I was naturally strong from all that work on the farm growing up, but in the long term it just wouldn't do.

Pat said it to me straight out. I was eleven and a half stone, and he said I'd need to get up to around 13 stone. And I knew it too.

If I was going to pick up some of the top forwards in the country, I'd need that extra stone and a half.

Pat was crucial to our gym work, though, because he ensured we did it properly. That's something that can't be overstated.

Sportspeople of all types hear nowadays about the benefits of doing an Olympic lift – a highly technical and challenging method of weight-lifting, which includes movements such as 'the snatch' and 'the clean and jerk' – say, but back then Pat had us doing the basics of that kind of lift, getting all the benefits of it without anyone getting injured. That's good going for a panel of 30 or 35 players.

The same with his sessions on the mechanics of running. Some lads would have been dubious about that, but not me. I found it fascinating, and I kept a notebook at home where I noted down everything we did in his sessions. I didn't know then that later I'd want to get into fitness or coaching, but every evening I'd make a note of the warm-up, the gym session or running session, the weights and the reps.

None of us questioned him, either. Pat was an unbelievable sprinter himself and our fitness in 2004, under his training and direction, had been terrific.

We knew that other teams were discovering the gym around that time – the northern teams had always been big believers in weight training – and we needed to embrace it as well if we wanted to go to another level. And we had no doubt that Pat was the man to take us there.

We fell back in for fitness tests in January, which is something every player wants to do well in. It was also a chance to have a look at some of the newer faces. I was thinking, *I know his name, he's a corner-back … this one's a wing-back.*

Part of your mind works that way: this guy is going to look for my jersey. Only natural. After all, the man whose place I'd taken had probably thought the same thing the first night he saw me come in through the dressing-room door, and he was absolutely right.

In training, Pat was central. He'd take the warm-up, then we'd play football, and then he'd take over after that for running.

One of Pat's specialities was the 'figure eight' run. We'd be running 150 metres almost without realising it because we were following a figure eight shape he'd marked out on the field with poles: a hard run from one corner of the pitch to the other, 100 metres, then a jog across of maybe 60 metres, then another 100 metres hard running.

It was game-specific, tailored to meet the demands of the game, and incorporated your recovery in the jogging – all the way back in 2005, which is fair credit to Pat.

Not everything was as modern. For instance, as a young lad you wouldn't dare go up on the masseur's table for a rub, even though it might have helped with the recovery. But having someone as professional as Pat involved was a lesson for the players – it showed that the setup was a serious one, based on science, and that sends a message. It underlines the professionalism in the camp, and that strengthens the self-belief among players.

It was a setup that had brought us to an All-Ireland in 2004 too, and that was in every player's head: the memories of coming home with the cup, the reception we'd got – that was all linked back to management.

Now, we also knew it was going to be tougher in 2005. Everything was ramped up. What had been an 80-metre run in 2004 would be 40 metres longer now, but we were prepared for that. We were ready.

Jack's approach in 2004 had been to take the league seriously, but there were one or two other significant factors. An Gaeltacht had made a run to the All-Ireland club final that year, which meant the Ó Sés, Dara Ó Cinnéide and the Mac Gearailts were unavailable for the county team.

That meant spots in defence that Tomás and Marc would normally take up were open.

Even as the league in 2005 progressed I could feel the benefits of the training. I was getting stronger, and the months that usually would have been a struggle for me with asthma, January and February, were in fact very productive for me.

And Pat was key to that also. He'd know if my breathing was hard and he'd encourage me just to get through it – and this at a time when there wouldn't be half as much contact or conversation between managers or coaches and players as there is nowadays. But he'd be very conscious that I might struggle if there was a heavy frost on a night we were training: the asthma was there, even though I had it largely under control. But Pat would make sure I got through the physical stuff and that I was right for the football part of training.

And despite all the focus on getting ourselves ready physically, that was the most important part of training – the ball work. It was simple in its own way, man on man in a game, with Jack roaring at the backs to get tighter.

There weren't any scenarios being rehearsed, no dropping wing-forwards back, or lining up with double sweepers, just a straight game between two teams, then a meal after training and gone.

There was a value to that, too, because the whole experience of training wasn't taking it out of you mentally. You went, you trained, you left: if you trained well, great, and if training didn't go well for you then you didn't think about it, you just aimed to do better at the next session.

Everything was geared towards the big internal game, which would be played on a Saturday, but even then there wasn't a sense of pressure there. It was enjoyable.

I was a different person too. I was young and full of beans, and I had an All-Ireland medal in my back pocket. I won't say it was a monkey off my back, but it was something I could point to. An achievement. And I wanted more medals to give some company to the one I had.

It didn't mean I was cocky in games from then on. I had a terrible obsession at the time with keeping my man from scoring.

But I also recognised what I could do and couldn't do. I wasn't going to be like Tomás or Séamus, bombing upfield or jinking through to get a point. If I went that far up the field my wings would be clipped fairly fast and I'd be sent back to my post. I had a job that I was good at, marking my man and hopefully keeping him scoreless, and I stuck to that.

The league games were enjoyable that spring and I put that down to my fitness. We'd trained into September the previous year and we had a good base of fitness from that, and on heavy pitches, with plenty of contact, I was in my element.

I was playing on the line, and by that I mean enjoying the physical contact.

And of course I enjoyed it because I was improving. I won't say it was coming easier to me, because it was still a test every day, but I was more experienced, I was maturing – I was nearly 25 – and I could get through the games in better shape.

What I couldn't do is get rid of people's preconceptions about me. I didn't have the pace Tom O'Sullivan had

– believe me, nobody had the pace Tom had – and that in turn led to people saying, 'Yeah, Mahony is strong but he's short a yard of pace.'

But as I pushed on I paid less and less attention to it.

The league was about holding onto the jersey. We'd heard that Séamus had gone away for the winter and had trained like the professional athlete he is in order to get himself right for 2005.

Which was great, but it was no help for me with the maths: seven players into six positions doesn't go. Tom, Marc and Mike Mac were terrific in the All-Ireland final, Tomás and Éamonn were on the team, and with Séamus coming back … My mind started drifting back to minor and under-21 days, and I was wondering if I'd be back on the bench.

A good league got me the start in the championship against Tipperary, though. I remember Jack saying to me before we went out, 'Don't worry about the ball. Follow your man everywhere he goes and if he doesn't score, that's your job done.'

He knew me inside out, how to get me tuned in, and I responded. We beat Tipperary and Limerick to qualify for the Munster final.

Cork in Cork, my first Munster final in Páirc Uí Chaoimh. That was a huge day for me, and not just because of the Cork–Kerry rivalry around the Rathmore area – though that was an element of it – but because I'd been to one Munster final before that as a spectator, and the atmosphere created by the Cork support was unreal. You had to take your hat off to them. It was phenomenal.

In the run-up to the 2005 game I remember lads in Kerry telling me the support would be four or five to one in favour of Cork, but I had enough on my plate.

I was picking up Donnchadh Walsh in training, and though he was a newcomer, in terms of energy and mobility he was the same at the start of his career as he was at the end: he never stopped running.

I was loving the battles at training with him, and at other times it was just a nightmare trying to stay with him, but it helped me too. My fitness was building again and mentally it was good preparation – hang in there, keep going, survive at all costs.

When the team was named for the Munster final Jack told me I was picking up Conor McCarthy. I could remember Conor playing with UCC and going on those long, long runs all over the pitch. He could pop up anywhere on the field, and he was one of the best half-forwards around because everything went through him for Cork as he was the link between the defence and the forwards. That was the game Cork played, and he facilitated that.

I could remember marking him in a college game: if I'd had a GPS on my back that day, my reading would have been very high in terms of distance covered. That kind of experience doesn't leave you.

In fairness to Jack, he'd thought it through and he spoke to me about it: 'You've spent a few evenings chasing Donnchadh Walsh, and that's the perfect preparation for Conor McCarthy. All we want is to stop him from getting the ball. Don't let him get the ball.'

He pointed out that, as Cork's main playmaker, Conor would drop deep and set up attacks, so I was to stay with him and blot him out of the game.

It revved up around Rathmore and Ballydesmond and Knocknagree for the few days beforehand. The Munster semi-final the year before was a home game, but this had a different edge to it, going to the enemy's den. People talk about All-Ireland finals, but growing up, the game for us was Cork and Kerry. Majestic games, and I was looking forward to this one, even though I was nervous as well.

The morning of the game we were waiting for Diarmuid Murphy to collect us at Mounthorgan Cross, near my house.

That's another big change in how teams prepare, by the way: nowadays you'd be heading off to a game at about eight in the morning and travelling by coach. That day myself and Tom were sitting on the wall for our lift beneath a life-size picture of the two of us, wishing us luck in the previous year's All-Ireland final.

We were wondering what was keeping Diarmuid – the most relaxed man of all time, he was probably watching *Soccer AM* on Sky Sports before heading out.

Cars were passing us, beeping to wish us good luck or roaring 'Up Cork' out the windows, and the two of us sitting in the sunshine, nearly 20 degrees already.

When Diarmuid arrived the car was already nearly full, and I sat on some fella's lap heading to the Munster final. Someone in the car said the temperature was supposed to hit 28 or 29 degrees by game time that afternoon, which wasn't news I welcomed. Not with the prospect of following Conor McCarthy for the entire match.

Back then, hydration wasn't top of anyone's to-do list either. If we stopped at a shop on the way, someone could have come out with crisps and a can of Coke. Professionalism was on the horizon but we hadn't quite reached it at that stage.

In the old Páirc Uí Chaoimh I always loved the dressing rooms, though lads sometimes complained about them. Fair enough, they were very tight, but I thought it just added to the occasion, even if you were in danger of a belt of a shoulder from one of your own players in the confined space.

It was a different experience: that time you'd hear the other crowd roaring in their dressing room, and they'd hear you – while I definitely got a belt of a shoulder running out onto the field that day because there were so many people in the tunnel.

People might forget now, but coming out of the old dressing rooms in the Páirc you ran across the tunnel

under the stands, so you'd get plenty of encouragement
– and the exact opposite – from people milling around.

When the ball was thrown in I suffered an early
setback, but I had learned from the previous year's All-
Ireland final to put the head down and plough on.

Derek Kavanagh won the throw-in for Cork and Conor
and I went around the middle to pick up the breaking
ball: I went for the ball and Conor ducked behind me,
then Derek set off with the ball, the two of them running
almost stride for stride together – they were so close they
bumped shoulders.

Derek won't give the ball to him, I thought.

Derek did give the ball to him, though, and Conor
McCarthy hit a good point off his left. Fourteen seconds
in.

Right, it's all about the next ball now. The temperature
was about 26 degrees, but less than a minute into the
game and I was feeling as if it was 36.

From then on Conor was everywhere on the field, just
a fantastic athlete that any team would be lucky to have.

Stick with it, I thought to myself. *Hang in there.* I
started to squeeze on him and won a couple of balls –
one ball came to Conor and he slipped and I picked it up
and laid it off, and that helped to settle me down.

By half-time he had a point kicked, which I wasn't
happy with – particularly after only 14 seconds – but it
was a reasonable return. Cork led us by a point.

The dressing room was like an oven with the heat. It was definitely 29 degrees on the field by that time and a good deal hotter inside. I just had my head down with a wet towel over it, hoping Conor would slow down in the second half.

After the break I won the first couple of balls and laid them off immediately with a hand-pass. It was drilled into me not to give away possession by chancing a kick-pass, but as the half wore on I came into it more. Both of us were tiring by then and I was checking his runs with my hands. Anything for a break.

Late in the game Tom O'Sullivan won the ball and came up the right wing before finding me with a hand-pass. I saw Declan O'Sullivan coming hard with his man on the inside 21.

And something popped into my head: Jack was always drilling into us that, if we had the chance in a game, we were to give a pass to the sideline side of a team-mate, in order to give him the chance to spin his man.

I gave the ball to the line side of Declan, he spun his man and went through for the goal.

That was a huge boost to me. I was crediting myself with an assist as though it was a fantasy football competition, but it was a crucial score as we won by three points.

It was a great win, but afterwards fellas were absolutely drained in the dressing room. Empty. That was the first time I really experienced that championship white heat. Whatever about league games, or even Munster championship games and All-Ireland semi-finals, this was a different level.

Cork had been hurt the year before and were building nicely. They put us to the pin of our collar to get over the line, and Conor's performance was a good example of that. He brought my game to a different level.

That can be a funny one. If you went up to some lads and said, 'Marking you brought me on to a different level,' they would take it as an insult, but I'd be genuine and mean it as a compliment.

Staying with Conor for 60 or 70 minutes that day brought me on, even though I'd be the first to say that if a bounce or two of the ball had gone his way I'd have a different perspective on it.

Going back to Killarney there was a huge sense of satisfaction for us. Beating Cork in a Munster final in Cork was serious business, and we celebrated it. That time you were allowed the Monday to enjoy a win, and on the Tuesday night you came back to training to be flogged around the field. We knew that was coming and submitted gladly. Back to business.

Facing into the All-Ireland series, I was pretty confident of holding onto the jersey, particularly as a defender. At that time if you were doing your job as a man-marker you were likely to hold your place. Up front the forwards needed to be scoring and creating, but a back's job was far more straightforward: keep your man from scoring, pure and simple.

We were playing Mayo in the All-Ireland quarter-final in Croke Park and my instructions were the same: 'Mark your man out of the game' – but if you did that properly you'd get on more ball anyway.

We got two goals that knocked them back, and towards the end Mike Mac and Séamus kicked points to drive us on.

Séamus in particular always seemed to chip in with a point or a run to lift the team, a driven player. Looking back, even then he was doing what coaches now preach all the time – that if you're a defender who beats his man to the ball and wins it, your job isn't even half-done. You have to do something constructive with it, to go on and be available for the out-ball then as well.

I was following Alan Dillon out the field as he went looking for the breaks, but when the ball came to Mike Frank Russell he looked around and gave it out to me.

Within scoring distance.

I could nearly feel the blood drain from my face as I kicked it. In training fellas would often chance kicking with the outside of the boot or trying to bend the ball in and out, but Jack wouldn't be long sending defenders like myself in behind the goal to kick the ball back out to the sharpshooters.

A bit more practice out in front of the goal would have made me more confident, but when I got the ball from Mike Frank I just put the boot through it – no subtlety, never mind using the outside of the boot – and over it went.

On the way back down the field the thought popped into my head: *I've kicked a point in Croke Park.* When I got back into the dressing room Jack said, 'That's your annual point scored now' – he wasn't planning on moving me up to replace the Gooch any time soon.

But I was walking on air leaving the dressing room. The point was the icing on the cake, and I noticed when I read the match reports in the papers the next day – which every player does, no matter what they might say – that a few commentators were saying I'd come of age, or added to my game, by kicking my first point.

When I got home I even noticed a change in my dad's approach to filling in the scrapbooks. He'd now included, on a new page, the little box that comes with the newspaper report detailing the scorers. So he'd snipped out the part saying 'A. O'Mahony (0–1)' and stuck it under a picture of me in action in the Mayo game.

The forwards didn't really need my support that year, but just to be sure I thought I'd show them the way in the semi-final against Cork as well, so I got up and hit the first point of the game. Just to help out.

Our form was good, particularly up front. Gooch was

flying, and so was Mike Frank. Declan O'Sullivan and Liam Hassett were outstanding. They were going so well it made our job as defenders much easier, because all we had to do was get the ball to them and they'd do the rest.

I was on Conor McCarthy again for the semi-final, though, and I soon had enough to be doing. There seemed to be a lot more terrain in Croke Park than in Páirc Uí Chaoimh, and we saw a lot of it, but I felt more confident than I had in the Munster final.

Having marked Conor I knew what his game was, what he'd be likely to do, and I squeezed him from the word go. It didn't affect his confidence, because he'd continue to make those runs, to make himself available and to win ball.

That was another element to my approach. When you mark a player like Conor he's going to get on the ball, and you have to accept that it's not a disaster if he does.

In the Munster final I tried to win absolutely every ball, but that's unrealistic: there were bound to be balls he'd win because of the quality of the pass or his positioning.

For the All-Ireland semi-final I accepted going in that he was going to win possession at times and there was nothing I could do about it – I just had to be in his face when he turned to look upfield, to make sure he passed the ball backwards and not set up the inside line.

I was reasonably happy that he wasn't setting up play or dictating the pace of the game. He dropped deep early on and I went with him, and that's how I ended up getting my point.

I got a ball from Cinnéide and came down the wing on the Hogan stand side and cut in, soloed off my left and realised I was only about 30 yards out so I turned onto my right and put it over the black spot into Hill 16.

I got a huge boost in confidence and it settled us as a team as well. We got into the game and it went well – we were on top at the back and the forwards started to cut loose.

At half-time we were 0–11 to 0–4 ahead and we finished 1–19 to 0–9: the benefit of a tough game against Mayo certainly stood to us. It set us up for another meeting with Tyrone, this time in the All-Ireland final.

I'd watched on as Tyrone had smothered Kerry in the 2003 All-Ireland semi-final, and now I'd be on the field. We were probably going into that game as favourites, given how well we'd played all year, how well our forwards were going.

But Tyrone were battle-hardened. They'd played nine games and had been able to get their line-up right. We felt we were ready, but so did they.

9

Tyrone in 2005

Lessons in Defeat

One of the key factors about 2005 was that, despite the newcomers, there were a lot of lads still on the panel from the famous day in 2003 when Tyrone had surprised Kerry in Croke Park. They were able to give us a first-hand account of the intensity Tyrone had brought that day, something we'd all seen as spectators.

Was it an opportunity for revenge? Not for me personally. As someone on the fringes of the panel it wasn't as immediate to me.

Was it for others? Of course it was, there's no point in denying that.

I'd have looked at where we were in 2003 and where we were in 2005 and I'd have been very confident. We had two good years of gym work under our belts in the meantime, and coming into the Tyrone game we would have worked very hard on moving the ball, moving the ball. Jack would have spoken about that constantly – not taking the ball into contact but moving it on as fast as we could.

I got the phone call from him a couple of weeks out from the final. The usual job – he was out walking up and down the mountains in south Kerry and was checking in with various players.

'How are you feeling?'

'Good.'

'You're in great shape and you've marked some of the best forwards in the country. The next day you'll be picking up Stephen O'Neill.'

'Right,' I said.

I knew well that O'Neill had scored 5–46 in the championship up to that point. The score was in my mind because it seemed any time I picked up a newspaper around then that number was being used, and Stephen O'Neill was already being talked up as a shoo-in for player of the year. The 5–46 he had in his back pocket was a powerful argument to support that view.

I had to sit down to get my head around it properly. What I'd seen of Stephen O'Neill was *The Sunday Game*, basically – video analysis wasn't as big a part of coaching as it is now – but I could see him in my mind's eye kicking points off his left, points off his right …

I started worrying. It was all very well to just stay with him, but I was thinking should Tom or Mike Mac or Marc be picking him up? Inside in training I'd be on Mike Frank or Cinnéide or Declan a few nights as Jack – cute as ever – started gearing me towards what I'd be up against. All different playing styles but they would all test you and therefore improve your defending skills.

At that point I'd nearly call it euphoria, the feeling around Kerry. At other times you could be waiting forever for payback against a team, and here we were two years later facing Tyrone after a big win over Cork and a good win over Mayo.

Now, we knew they'd had big tests, that they had an unbelievable team. That's not just *plámás*: look at the players they had out that day, and the forwards in particular: Brian McGuigan centre-forward and Peter Canavan full-forward. Stephen O'Neill, Mellon, Brian Dooher, Mulligan. Not bad.

I'd have been a good man for looking at the newspapers in the run-up to a big game like that, and not a single one had picked me out to mark Stephen O'Neill.

I could understand the thinking – here was an array of marquee forwards, and anyone would want their most experienced defenders to match up with them. But in my own mind I knew I was picking up the most in-form attacker in the country. That was what I'd call an expression of faith by a manager.

The build-up was huge. It's an All-Ireland football final, and no matter who's involved it's a big deal, obviously, but everything seemed to be focused on the Kerry–Tyrone rivalry – and managing your energy in particular.

Thankfully there was no such thing as social media to contend with. There was an open day, a press day – I don't think I even spoke to the media because Jack would be saying, 'Take this man out of that equation anyway.' Being a young fella there was enough pressure going into a game without worrying about what you said in the papers in the lead-up, but there wouldn't have been orders from management about our approach to the media.

We would have been told to stay out of town or to stay at home and avoid people because you didn't want to be drained by questions about the match for the whole week beforehand.

In later years that would change a little, but at the time, I felt it was nearly counter-productive because you were avoiding people so much that the prospect of the game could play on your mind regardless and drain you anyway.

It was a different world, though. Looking back now, the team wouldn't have been named at that stage and there might be a couple of hundred people in Fitzgerald stadium watching us train or play a practice match (and filming it all for consumption north of the border, I've no doubt).

It's funny to look back at that now, because a fella's form in training was no secret at all. I often went back to Rathmore after Kerry training and I might meet someone there who could tell me Mike Frank had kicked two points off me an hour earlier inside in the stadium. The story often beat me out the road to Rathmore.

We learned that anyone could walk in and see what way the team was lining up and what tactics were being used, and the gates were closed after, but we lost something when that happened too, even though it was necessary. There would have been great characters in watching the training – the likes of Jimmy O'Brien, owner of Jimmy Brien's Bar, a Killarney native who had been to every All-Ireland and every training session, Ambrose O'Donovan or the late Weeshie Fogarty, the man whose commentary on Radio Kerry made you feel like you were actually at the game, and there'd be a bit of banter with them or encouragement from them, to be fair.

My biggest goal in the run-up was to find some kind of an angle. Somebody might ask why I'd need that for a game as big as Kerry–Tyrone, and it's a complicated one.

I might back myself to mark Stephen O'Neill, but was I confident? No. And if I heard someone say, 'Well, he won't be picking up O'Neill anyway,' it might get into my head.

In that situation a player needs reassurance. Jack spoke to me one-on-one the night before: 'You're having a great year – you're well able.'

Although there were a lot of similarities to the build-up to 2004 – though I slept a little better in 2005 – there was a different atmosphere. We were hearing about the battle for tickets and the game was being described as the perfect final.

The nerves were there on the way in, but I was able to work on that: I remember saying to myself, *You wanted to be there in 2003, now you are here. You can't be saying you'd prefer to sit back in the dressing room; there's a responsibility on you and you know what it's like to have the back of your net rattled in the first few minutes of an All-Ireland final, so whatever comes at you you'll be prepared for it.*

I have a strong memory from before the game: it's funny what comes into your mind when you get out onto the field and the sound swallows you up. In 2004 my thoughts were revolving around meeting the president and walking around behind the band and what that would feel like, what the colours up on the Hill would look like.

In 2005, though, I was thinking about people's reaction when they saw me walking over to pick up Stephen O'Neill in the full-back line. When I did, Tom went on Canavan and Mike Mac picked up Mulligan.

We shook hands. The ball was thrown in.

Tyrone started off playing into the Hill 16 end, which was full of their own supporters, and obviously the Tyrone management didn't have the same faith in me that Jack did, because the first chance Tyrone got, they hit a long one in on top of myself and O'Neill, obviously trying to get him into the game early.

The ball came in high, but just high enough – it carried over his head and I caught it and landed with it, and I remember the thought flashed into my mind – *It's there, it's in my hand* – before I got it away.

The game took off, and he got on the ball – and on the ball in dangerous areas; he was too good a player not to be involved. But my focus was to make it to half-time and not let him score.

To do that we had to squeeze them, to follow our men, and when you do that you're going to get on the ball yourself, even as a defender. You had to be an outlet because Tyrone were going to tackle us in threes and fours, and we knew that.

Early on we gave up turnover after turnover, though – it was as though we'd forgotten about the basics, if that makes sense. People associate Kerry football with being slick, but we weren't slick.

Before the break I was coming out and burst past two Tyrone players – but the third player stripped the ball from me.

That intensity they brought was a level above what we had encountered from other teams, despite the fact that we'd spoken about that specifically before the game. We felt that if there were three players around one of us, then another team-mate had to be free nearby, but Tyrone had prepared it so well, they'd obviously practised it so much that they trusted each other to tackle in twos and threes, and that cut down our passing outlets.

We felt we had a bit about us, though. We had the work put in, and Gooch got us off to a great start, kicking a brilliant point from out near the Cusack stand.

He helped to set up Dara Ó Cinnéide's goal as well, but then he was on the ground. Someone caught him in the eye and he was down for a good while.

Even so, we were going well. We had a goal, we were moving the ball, it was all going to plan.

Then one of our lads was turned over out on the sideline and they pumped a high ball in on top of Owen Mulligan, who caught it.

I'd still have flashbacks about that passage of play, Canavan coming around the corner for the pass – you could tell even as it was happening in front of you that it had been practised over and over again. He took the ball and rolled it into the corner.

It wasn't a killer blow, because it was too soon in the game for that, but it was still a sickener, coming against the run of play.

We'd been going so well that you could measure it. To this day if I'm talking to players I tell them they'll always know when they're really rolling in a game, because the opposition crowd is quiet. And we'd quietened the Tyrone support that day.

People might say the crowd doesn't have an impact on the game, but they're wrong: when you're going well and your own crowd are roaring you on the confidence rises; your tails are up. (We had the same experience in 2011 against Dublin, but in reverse – their crowd was quiet until late on, and then they really got behind the Dubs.)

When you break it down, that goal had two classic ingredients. First, Mulligan's great hands, so quick, and his unselfishness, giving it to Canavan when he saw him coming around on the loop.

And then for Canavan, who's God almighty in Tyrone, to get the goal – against the run of play, against Kerry, into the Hill with thousands of Tyrone supporters willing it into the net in front of them.

Brian McGuigan got a massive point just after that: he checked, stood and hit it over at an almighty height, and it was a fair swing. We had been ahead with half-time approaching but we went in three points down instead.

And that's where the crowd comes in, because the Tyrone support roared them in at half-time.

When you look back now, they had been hardened

in the championship: they'd been through far tougher battles than us along the way and being in a battle against us was no hardship for them. They were well used to it at that stage.

In fairness, though, we were settled enough at half-time. Jack got us to sit down and went through some simple messages: take your points. Settle yourselves. Get back into the game.

There was another strong message – that we were in the game, and that we had brought a lot of the trouble on ourselves through turnovers rather than being beaten all over the field.

For myself, I had kept O'Neill scoreless from play and the other defenders had done well too: we had been under the cosh for a lot of the first half but in general we'd held them out.

When we went back out, though, Tyrone got a couple of early points and then we were chasing the game. O'Neill still hadn't scored and I was telling myself not to switch off, but he got a ball and went down the Cusack stand side.

I was thinking, *He's going to turn back in on his right here because it's not a left-footed kick.* And then of course Stephen O'Neill did what Stephen O'Neill could do – 40 yards out, bang, over the bar. He gave me a thump of a shoulder coming back out. After hitting a point like that, he was entitled to it.

What I notice looking back is that we seemed to be tackling in groups ourselves, particularly in that second half – if a defender was caught, someone was there to support him almost immediately. I got a bit of help a couple of times myself and was grateful for it.

The intensity was non-stop; the running and tackling never slackened: it was at a different level to the previous year, even. Tyrone's conditioning, their tackling, their hitting was unbelievable – and in fairness we were matching them. I can remember coming out with a couple of balls and when I gave them off I was winded – but you couldn't go down for a breather. You wouldn't let yourself be seen to take a breather.

They were still ahead when Tomás Ó Sé intervened. He just had that capability, that engine, to range upfield at times – but he had that beautiful kicking style as well. In the Munster final that year he kicked two screamers of points, and against Tyrone he drove up again late on as though he was going to do the same.

This time, though, there were a couple of rebounds and deflections before the ball broke to him, but he had the presence of mind to rattle the net and leave a couple of points in it. We went for broke and tried to break them down, and they retreated back the field. Late on, Canavan nearly took Gooch's jersey off as Tyrone were holding out, but if the situation was reversed you'd be as quick to do the same. No complaints.

Looking back on it, at the final whistle the supporters in white jerseys were streaming past, the odd one bumping and shoving – but I took it all in. I took in the hurt, the feeling.

Coming in under the Hogan stand I can remember someone – a supporter, one of theirs – saying I'd done a great job on O'Neill, holding him to two points. 'Are you for real?' I said.

It was the wrong thing to say – the man was probably just trying to find a positive for me – but I was broken-hearted, like the rest of the lads. It was my first time feeling that real sense of loss, something I wouldn't want to feel too often in my life.

In the dressing room there wasn't a word, but the noise of cheering seeped through from outside. I flashed back to 2004 and the joy we'd felt at that moment, but the scenario 12 months later had me thinking, *How do we get out of this? How am I going to face the Kerry supporters?*

We'd given it everything. We'd made mistakes, and we'd probably let the game slip away, but that's not an excuse. I always hold to the line that the team that wins a game is the team that deserves to win the game. They might need a bit of luck to win, but that doesn't make it a lucky win.

You have to go into the players' lounge after the All-Ireland final, and again, it's a very different experience when you lose. You're 10 feet tall when you walk in after winning, but after losing you just want to hide away in the corner with your family.

And the doubts start. You start thinking, *Am I going to be involved next year? Is this lad next to me going to be involved next year? Will we get back?*

The negativity that comes from losing is huge, and that's before I even considered the bus journey back to the hotel, the dinner, watching *The Sunday Game*, all of that.

After an All-Ireland final the supporters come in their droves to the team hotel, win or lose, and after the meal I'd always leave the function and go out to thank them, to say a few words from the stage.

But when you lose, the supporters are heartbroken for the players, the players' families are heartbroken for the players, the players are heartbroken themselves.

It's funny that everything that is enjoyable when you win, you want to avoid when you lose. There's no-one in the hotel lobby looking to talk to you the following morning, the train journey back to Kerry is a long one, the fatigue is setting in because your mind is in a very negative place.

Stopping in Rathmore, though, we saw the greatness of the GAA. The crowd was the same as it was the previous year even though we'd lost.

They were trying to give us a lift, to let us know they appreciated what we'd done. And by doing that they did

Playing with Rathmore Under-14s. I was twelve years old in this photo, on the back row, third from the right.

Playing senior with Rathmore. I was around eighteen years old in this picture. There is such a sense of community and pride with club football.

One of the most successful Rathmore teams in the O'Donoghue cup, winning four in a row.

This photo was taken in 2006. One of the best things about playing football was how proud my parents were of me and the enjoyment they got out of it.

Running out for the Australian International Rules First Test
in Pearse Stadium Galway, 28 October 2006.

What happened that day in 2008 is something
I'll always regret. It had a huge impact on me
but I've learned that the only thing you can do is
learn and move on from your mistakes.

I came back to playing with a different mindset. I was still as focused as I'd always been but was more centred and happy in myself.

■ FALLEN IDOL: Rathmore's Aidan O'Mahony under pressure from Laune Rangers' Liam Hassett in the Kerry SFC clash in Beaufort.
Picture: Eamonn Keogh /MacMonagle, Killarney.

O'Mahony makes return as Rathmore sneak thriller

Kerry SFC

Rathmore	2-11
Laune Rangers	2-8

Ciaran McCarthy

AIDAN O'MAHONY marked his return to football in some style as Rathmore scored two late late goals to seal a last-gasp victory against Laune Rangers in a cracking second round Kerry County Senior Football Championship tie in

club and he was one of the best performers as they staged a dramatic comeback to secure victory.

The game was held up for eight minutes following an injury to Rathmore sub Daniel O'Sullivan in the second half, and in time added on, Rathmore's super sub John Moynihan popped up with two superb goals.

Suddenly, from trailing 2-7 to 0-10, Rathmore jumped ahead as Moynihan struck twice in two minutes for the East Kerry club.

It was hard luck on Rangers as ...

Late in the first half, Rangers' Shane McSweeney scored a fine team goal to give his side a 1-4 to 0-6 advantage, though the Killorglin side, who were missing Mike Frank Russell through injury, should have been further ahead.

After a Peter Crowley score for Rangers early in the second half, Rathmore came back with a fine Aidan O'Mahony point and a John Buckley free to level the game, 0-8 to 1-5.

Rangers had edged in front once more, 1-7 to 0-9, before Kevin Flynn struck for his side's second goal, and leading by four points, it seemed like

for those two late goals that earned a superb win for Rathmore.

RATHMORE: J Cooper; M O'Sullivan, T O'Sullivan, J O'Sullivan (0-1); C Kelly, K Cahill, B O'Leary; A O'Mahony (0-1), J Buckley (0-1 free); M Reen (0-3), D Hayes; D O'Keeffe, D O'Sullivan, M O'Riordan (0-3 frees), P Murphy, P Reen (0-1).

Subs: Daniel O'Sullivan for Donal O'Sullivan (ht); S Lehane for Daniel O'Sullivan (inj) (53k); J Moynihan (2-0) for M O'Riordan

LAUNE RANGERS: T Lyons; J Carey, C Sheehan, C Riordan; P Crowley (0-1), Coffey, K Crowley; J Lynch, S Foley; T McSweeney (1-1), P Joy (0-1), M Foley; Doona (0-1), L Hassett (0-2, 0-1 free), Flynn (1-2, 0-1 free).

The All-Ireland semi-final in 2013. I'd dislocated my elbow and broken two bones in it while training ahead of the Munster Senior Final just five weeks beforehand. I'd vowed to myself that I'd win an All-Ireland for my dad and I'd done everything I could that year despite the injury. It wasn't to be but I was determined to try again in 2014.

Looking up to my dad as I lift the Sam Maguire in 2014,
knowing that I'd fulfilled my promise to him to win an All-Ireland.

Overwhelmed by our win, knowing that everyone involved
had given it everything.

The Sam Maguire coming back
to Rathmore.

From left to right: Paul Murphy,
Maurice Joe O'Connor, myself
and Shane Ryan.

Denise and I got married in the Algarve, August 2015.

Me with my mam at my wedding.

Lilah (left) and Lucia (right).

One of our annual trips with Denise's family.

Proudly holding the *Dancing with the Stars* trophy in 2017, with my dance partner Valeria Milova.

Myself, Dayl and Des Cahill.

With my business partner at AOM Fitness, Michael O'Donoghue.

Denise and I walking the Portuguese Camino in 2019. I went as an ambassador for CRY (Cardiac Risk in the Young).

I started running in 2018, realising that I could look beyond my football bubble. Here I am taking part in the Rose of Tralee 10K.

Swimming was a real fear for me and I'm still nervous in the water but I try to set goals for myself and overcoming my fear was one of them. Fenit, County Kerry, August 2020.

gave us a lift and made us all the more determined to get back again.

In a blink of an eye, a year goes by. The same date, the same venue ... the only difference is the result.

The silence is deafening from the minute you enter the dressing room under the Hogan stand. It's like a bad dream, but there's no getting away from this one – you need to go through the pain, the pain of the aftermath, the what-ifs.

The first few days are raw – everyone reacts differently to a loss, but you can't comprehend disappointment like that unless you experience it.

I took defeat really badly, but you can work it to your advantage and push yourself even more for the following season. In life you need to see the bottom before you can get back up, and that setback made me more determined than ever to get back out there. And win.

10

The Donncha O'Connor Affair

From my first training session with Kerry until my last, as soon as I walked in the door at home afterwards the details of the session were jotted down in a notepad. My thinking back then was simple: if I noted down the details, I could do the session again by myself in the days I wasn't in training with Kerry. No such thing as recovery days back then.

My note-taking, like the training sessions themselves, has evolved over time. These days I write up the sessions noting any times, distances, weights, sets and reps, but I also give myself little pointers – noticing what wasn't going well and setting myself targets for improvement.

My note-taking didn't end there. When you have a dad that records every televised game you play, you have video analysis up and running long before the days of dedicated statisticians.

In 2008 I had left out no details – every distance, time, rep recorded, every game broken down, play by play. But there was one game where the details were noticeably different. The All-Ireland semi-final against Cork.

We'd been beaten by Cork in the Munster final and found ourselves travelling the qualifier route, with hard-fought wins against Monaghan and Galway, so we were more than primed for the rematch with our neighbours.

Cork were ready for this one as well. We had beaten them in the previous year's All-Ireland final, and the hurt they felt, mixed with the confidence of beating us only six weeks previously, brought out something different in them.

In the Munster final, Cork had set up with a runner at centre-forward, dragging me all over the place; but the semi-final tactics were different.

Pearse O'Neill, Graham Canty and Alan O'Connor made up their middle third, all over six feet tall, all lining up with the intention of running straight and laying down a marker.

Leading up to that game I'd already marked John Miskella of Cork (a runner), Monaghan's Rory Woods (a battering ram) and Galway's Pádraic Joyce (a superstar).

I'd acquitted myself well, so when Pearse O'Neill came jogging over, all six feet five of him, I met him head on. Pearse had the same approach and we spent a couple of minutes getting to know each other before any ball was thrown in.

Looking back now, my notepad paints my performance:

> 0:06   Catch the breaking ball punched from the throw-in (stay switched on from start)
> 0:50   Cork first attack – long, high ball (need to be closer to full-back line)
> 11:22   Get on the end of move – carry – kick a wide from 21 (right foot, practise left)
> 14:00   P. O'Neill wins a free, gives one-two, sets up goal (don't switch off)
> 16:17   Catch a break, deliver 30-yard pass to running forward (more of this)

After 22 minutes Pearse was moved out to midfield and Nicholas Murphy came off the bench to move on to me at centre-forward. Nicholas greeted me with a shoulder instead of a neighbourly handshake: no surprise there.

At this point the middle third was a real battleground, Cork had flooded it with big men, all the time trying to isolate Darragh Ó Sé by having Alan O'Connor run him to the sideline.

Leaving Graham Canty, Pearse O'Neill and myself and Séamus Scanlon to battle it out.

That battle ramped up a notch after 37 minutes when Darragh got sent off. What had been our middle third was now up for grabs, and the Cork lads knew it.

We knew it too, which was the strength of that 2008 team. The obvious didn't need to be pointed out to us – we took action ourselves.

Kieran Donaghy came out of the full-forward line into midfield, Declan O'Sullivan started sweeping deeper, picking up break after break. The boys were turning up the performance and everyone was feeding off it.

In those circumstances there isn't much that has to be said. The cues come from the body language or a glimpse of the two boys' faces. If you weren't sprinting into breaks before, the shackles were now fully off and the what-ifs were forgotten – it was all about getting the ball or clearing out that red jersey near the ball.

The tempo was set; our forwards were at full tilt. My job was simple: get the ball and get it in to them.

The last entry from my notepad is '48:45 – delay & dispose Ger Spillane'. What followed probably took me the best part of two years to get over.

After I met Ger Spillane by the sideline, the ball spilled out and off the pitch. My team-mate Killian Young collected the ball and looked to move it into the forwards straight away: as he did so, Cork's Donncha O'Connor tried to slow the process, attempting to block the pass.

Without thinking, I cleared Donncha out of the way, with both of us falling against the small barrier that separates the crowd from the pitch. With the crowd literally on our backs, Donncha and I squared off, neither of us taking a backward step.

The linesman came in to separate us and when he did so Donncha reached out and slapped my face.

I fell to the ground, clutching my face to make it obvious to all that there was a strike. After a quick debate with his linesman, the referee sent Donncha off.

The whole thing, from getting slapped on the face to falling down and getting back up again, lasts four seconds. They're like every other second in a game, with the focus moving swiftly onto the next second, the next ball.

The game ended badly for us: we were six points up going into the last minute of the game and it should have been job done, but out of nowhere Cork got a goal and then a penalty. Draw. We would go to a replay.

Walking off the pitch after a game like that, you just want to get into the changing room, get your things, get on the bus and get home. Reflecting on the game can wait.

This time it was different.

I turned my phone on when leaving the changing room and saw a text:

> I wouldn't be going on social media there for a while, they're after cutting the back off you on RTÉ.

On the bus to the station nobody was speaking because of how the game ended. My phone started to ping as one by one messages came in, all of them with a view on the incident.

On the train down it was the same: people who I didn't even realise had my number soon felt it was necessary for me to hear their opinion.

To make matters worse, my quads started to cramp up, and I had to get towels wrapped around my legs for the pain all the way down. But if I thought that journey was bad, the next few days brought it all home to me.

I was 28, and while finding my feet at centre-back with Kerry, my non-footballing career was on a similar trajectory: I had joined An Garda Síochána in 2004 and was by then a fully qualified member of the force.

That year I was stationed in Anglesea Street, the biggest station in Cork city, and that Monday, following the game, I was on the public desk. And the very first person who came to the hatch, to get their passport stamped or whatever business they had, recognised me.

'You should be ashamed of yourself,' he said.

And I was. I was thoroughly ashamed of myself.

At lunch time I took a walk out to stretch the legs and on passing the local shop I saw the front page of one of the newspapers: a photo of me on the ground and the word CHEAT headlined above.

When I watched the incident back my own reaction was certainly along the lines of, *Christ, what were you thinking?*

In Kerry there are unwritten rules, standards set by those gone before. I was the kid up on the shoulders of my dad looking to get a glimpse at returning Kerry teams: was this the standard they set? Was this how they held themselves?

These thoughts were constant in the days following the game. I didn't need external voices to tell me that what I had done was wrong. Trying to deal with my own thoughts was enough.

On the train home from the match the main thought was *How can I face this?* and that continued throughout the week. We met as a team a couple of days after the draw for a recovery session, and straight afterwards there was an interview for Pat O'Shea, our manager: I was apologising for the incident. In the days afterwards I knew Pat would have to face the media for my antics on the pitch.

It was a difficult situation for me, but also a situation that Pat didn't need to find himself in. An unwanted distraction. But Pat – as Pat does – dealt with it coolly and calmly, stepping up and speaking first, with nothing but support for me personally, despite my wrongdoing. (I couldn't speak more highly of Pat O'Shea; in his two years in charge of Kerry I learned so much from him and his coaching methods. He's a massive family- and clubman, and he was always approachable with every player – and he wasn't found wanting when I needed him most, something I will always be grateful to him for. He has guided his club to All-Ireland success and he coaches all the underage teams with his club every Saturday morning. He's a role model for me as an aspiring coach.)

I apologised and said that Donncha had had nothing at all to do with it, that he should be allowed to play in the replay. The interview lasted about five minutes. But it had felt like five hours.

With age comes maturity, something I didn't have back then. It was a difficult time, but I faced every challenge head on – the public apology, going out in public despite the constant reminders … The easy option would have been to shy away from it. I believe that stubbornness not to let it defeat me was ingrained in me from a young age, possibly because of dealing with the asthma.

The replay came four days later. In the warm-up, the teams were announced in the stadium, and when my name was read out over the tannoy the boos rang out. A full house in Croke Park creates its own unique atmosphere, and you are very much aware of the buzz of the crowd when you are on the pitch.

But the other side of that also holds, and there was no getting away from the boos that day.

I got through the full game – which we won – but looking at my notepad I had eight possessions, all laid off with a hand-pass. I was playing within myself.

I wish it hadn't happened, of course, but I can't change that. I've spoken with Donncha about it personally and we've moved on from it.

Every now and again a reminder of the incident appears, usually a clip of the dive on social media. I put up a Q&A box every Thursday night on my business (AOM Fitness) Instagram account where people can type in questions for me to answer. I'm asked about the incident every so often and in the limited time or space I have to answer I can only say, 'It happened and I can't do anything to change it; don't let incidents like that define you, learn from your mistakes and move on.'

Rumination can be dangerous. That's the biggest lesson I took from the incident. I've learned that you are much better off reviewing what happened, noting your mistake, recognising where you can improve and moving on.

Another lesson I learned was that you can't always take things on by yourself. I was very fortunate that the support network I had at that time was incredible – my family, my team-mates, my work colleagues. No matter what the scenario was, there was always someone pulling me aside, asking, 'Are you okay?'

In truth, I wasn't.

It's one of the biggest lessons I've learned. I played 'on the line' in football terms, and when you're involved in an incident like that you'd better be prepared for the backlash.

It seemed never-ending and eventually took its toll. It was in my mind for a long time that the incident would define me, and people were quick to tell me the same when it suited them.

I've made plenty of mistakes in my life. In the aftermath of this incident I held my hand up and apologised. The hardest part is that it happened with a player I would have grown up playing against all through my career, a guy I have massive respect for both on and off the pitch.

I would love to turn back the clock but I can't: I had my light-bulb moment; I owned it. It took time to move on as I was always reminded of it, but I'm not the only person to have made a mistake in life and be judged for that one moment.

Hence I'll always have a hand out to pick someone up when they need it, instead of kicking them when they're down. Because nobody ever really knows what is going on in another person's life.

11

A Test, a Ban, a Reprieve

When will this all stop? In 2008 I had the diving incident; afterwards we reached the All-Ireland final but lost to Tyrone. Seven weeks after that I was representing my country as part of the International Rules series against Australia in the MCG stadium in Melbourne, in front of thousands of Irish people living in Oz. A real career highlight. Two weeks after that I was standing in front of some of the same GAA officials I travelled with on that International Rules trip, waiting to find out if I'd be suspended from the sport I love because of a failed drugs test.

A rollercoaster of a season.

I started 2008 playing some of the best football of my career. I had cemented myself at centre-back and felt I was finding my feet in a team full of leaders. The Donncha O'Connor incident happened. I addressed it. I lost my second All-Ireland final but picked myself up and got straight back into training.

The reward was tangible. As part of representing Ireland in the International Rules series, I had the opportunity to train under Sean Boylan – and a serious back room. Seven weeks of hard training before we flew out for Australia, including a training camp in Toulouse, France. Full-time training. For that short period it was the closest thing to being a professional, full-time athlete, and I was in dreamland. It felt amazing, and it was a real distraction from the events of the previous summer.

The team is made up of players from different counties, and there were a lot of Cork lads, including Graham Canty, Pearse O'Neill and John Miskella.

Those guys were able to leave behind what had happened on the pitch that summer, and that was another help. I wasn't spared at the training sessions before we went out, though – there was plenty of craic between the players – but all in all, it was exactly what I needed.

I'd played in the 2006 series against Australia up in Pearse stadium in Galway and in Croke Park. That doesn't sound too long ago, but at that point GAA teams were still getting to grips with the gym and conditioning culture. There were a few 'getting to know you' incidents throughout that series and a few off-the-ball rather than on-the-ball clashes.

(Myself and Paul Galvin found ourselves on the

same wing, so at least we each had back-up whatever happened.)

Those tussles were one thing, but I can also remember putting everything into each 50/50 challenge and the Australians were well able to take it. Their conditioning was phenomenal.

Those games were fairly rough and questions were asked as to whether the series should continue. Because of that there was quite a focus on the 2008 series: we were well warned by the GAA that any nonsense off the ball wouldn't be accepted, with suggestions that bans earned in Australia would be carried over to the club and county seasons back home.

In an effort to keep everyone on the straight and narrow, the GAA and the Australian Football League (AFL) set up a 'meet and greet' evening on the night before the first test. I think on paper the idea was to get familiar with the other team and to make sure no bad blood was left from the 2006 series.

At the end of the night, there was a Champions League-style situation where both teams lined up to shake hands with each other, passing down the line.

Now, one player I'd had a couple of close encounters with in the 2006 series – especially in Croke Park – was Matthew Lappin, who was now an Australian selector. I had a feeling he hadn't forgotten me, a feeling that strengthened when I got a couple of Aussie handshakes that were on the firm side, put it that way. Matthew might have had a word in a couple of lads' ears, but I was no shrinking violet myself. I returned the handshakes with interest.

Being away from home for that period was refreshing; I was soaking up the professional lifestyle, seeing the level you could bring your fitness to. I was constantly learning.

I remember we were invited down to one of the Aussie Rules stadiums to see the setup a day or two before we played there, and on the tour of the stadium I could pick out one guy down on the pitch running laps.

I just kept watching him set off on his run – he was doing what must have been 3-kilometre time trials, over and over again. There was no-one around to encourage him, no crowd to feed off, no coach or other players to push him on: he was doing it all himself, the discipline and drive all his own.

Their game wasn't that different from ours after all. It still boiled down to the work you put in yourself.

I left Australia that October ready to leave 2008 behind and start afresh, beginning with my own training and bringing that to a different level.

On 17 November the GAA released a statement saying that an unnamed player had supplied a positive drugs test. Players can be tested at training and after games when a urine sample is taken by someone from the GAA or WADA, the World Anti-Doping Agency.

That morning I got a text message telling me my name had been leaked: that I had been revealed as the unnamed player.

Reading that kind of message sends all sorts of thoughts through your head. You think of the consequences. Of losing your job, the reactions of your friends, your family.

The immediate question – how did this happen? – doesn't even arise because the shock and the emotion are overwhelming.

I'd just finished a night shift with the guards and my plan for the day was to head up to Thomond Park for Munster versus the All Blacks with Ollie Favier and Michael Anthony Kelleher.

Instead my phone was hopping. I woke up in a panic, thinking that I had slept in, but when I looked at the phone I saw 89 missed calls, all backed up by text messages.

> You'll be named today as failing a drugs test

> You'll have to come out and give your side of the story

Variations on a theme.

The messages and calls kept coming through from lads I'd played with and against and journalists. To this day what doesn't sit right with me was people texting me to talk to this journalist or that journalist – or not to talk to this one or that one. All looking for an insight.

I don't know if it was a stubbornness not to shy away from it, but in the end I decided to head off to Limerick to the rugby match with the lads as planned.

Along the way I got a taste of the scale of the problem. We pulled in for a drink in Clem Smith's pub when we got to Limerick, and the six o'clock news came on the television, on the big screen. Breaking sports news, a GAA player has failed a drugs test: 'Aidan O'Mahony of Kerry—'

The bar was packed because of the rugby game, and I could see people begin to turn around and nudge each other and point and say, 'There he is, right there.'

How could you explain yourself to a packed bar? If ever I wanted a hole in the ground to open up and swallow me, that was the time.

That Munster–All Blacks game might go down in history, but to this day I can't tell you one passage of play. I was there in person but my mind was elsewhere. The game was a blur.

In the days that followed I was advised to get in touch with Paul Derham, a solicitor in Cork who's well known in rugby circles – and who'd represented Munster's Frankie Sheahan when he'd faced charges similar to mine.

I knew Paul from working in the courthouse in Cork, and the first day I walked into his office he just told me to give him my side of the story.

He put me completely at my ease and was fantastic to deal with from start to finish.

Going to see him indicated to me how serious it was, but that lesson was sinking in anyway: the papers had photographs of me with 'O'Mahony fails drugs test' as a caption on the front page.

When I saw those papers delivered into my place of work it brought home the seriousness of the issue all over again. Thankfully, at work the whole situation was dealt with professionally: I explained my side of the story, and I got nothing but support in return.

Outside, it was a different story. It was a media frenzy. I could understand that, but what really annoyed me was that my name had been leaked.

That anger was compounded when I saw reports that I'd get a two-year ban, as though I'd already been found guilty without any due process.

On top of everything else, I'd been advised to say nothing, which was probably good advice at the time – but it had the effect of maybe making me look guilty.

Silence can be interpreted in a lot of different ways, and there were those who were happy to interpret my silence as confirmation of my guilt.

In my daily work I met plenty of people who were not shy about making a comment about it, but I'd have felt that after the diving incident sympathy for me would have been in short supply anyway, so I buttoned my lip.

On 21 November I received a temporary ban until the hearing took place, and with no inter-county action to occupy people's attention at that time of year, there was no shortage of commentary about my case in the papers and on radio and television.

It affected me. I have no problem saying that. If I thought the week of the Donncha O'Connor incident was bad, having to explain myself every single day was draining.

The case never seemed to conclude. The first hearing with the GAA's anti-doping committee was fixed for 17 December in Dublin and one of my strongest memories of the whole experience was ringing the hotel where the meeting was taking place and asking them if I could get changed there beforehand.

The hotel staff went on and on about charging for this room and for that amount of time, and I was so keen to get it over with that I paid them for the night, even though I only needed five minutes to change my clothes.

Myself, Paul Derham and a doctor he enlisted were at the hearing, as was Dr Mike Finnerty, the Kerry team doctor, and Jerome Conway, the Kerry county board chairman. We were up before the GAA's Anti-Doping Committee, which included a former GAA president, a doctor and a QC.

Paul's instructions to me were simple: 'Just tell them what you told me in the office that day.'

That was great to hear, as opposed to a lawyer saying, 'Don't say this and don't mention that.'

At the meeting, Paul spoke, and then I was asked to speak.

I told the committee that I'd been an asthmatic for over 20 years, and that it was routine for me to use the inhaler every night before I went to bed.

With the nerves of a day like an All-Ireland final weighing on you it wouldn't be unusual to wake up at three in the morning and to take a few puffs of it. I'd used it that morning before the game and during the game: I told them exactly how many times I'd used it.

I also pointed out that my name had been leaked, and that my anonymity was gone, but I also acknowledged that it was up to me to be aware of the guidelines when it came to salbutamol, the active ingredient in the inhaler.

Players get a therapeutic form at the start of the year and fill it out, and I'd stated on my form that I used the inhaler two to three times a day.

I told the committee that when I use my inhaler, I take two puffs each time and when they asked why I hadn't clarified that and written that down, I accepted that that was my fault – that I should have done so, but that that was what I had been doing for the previous 20 years or so.

The hearing committee accepted my testimony completely. There was no apparent agenda and they took everything I said on board.

But then the whole thing was adjourned until after Christmas as they deliberated on it.

No result.

That kept the process going into the new year, which meant that with the national leagues on the horizon and training due to resume, I was left in limbo.

The energy and drive I'd had to return to training after the Australia trip were gone, and it was a tough few weeks.

I waited and waited for the hearing's outcome, constantly chasing county board officers for an update. I couldn't even think about finding closure until the final verdict came out on 22 January.

I remember reading the committee's conclusion that I hadn't been trying to enhance my performance but had taken the salbutamol while using my inhaler.

I'd expected that finding, but it was still a relief.

In all the years I'd played, I'd have taken a few puffs of the inhaler if I'd felt a bit wheezy, as anyone who's asthmatic would do.

I didn't know there was a threshold to the amount of salbutamol you were allowed to have in your system, and that was my fault. I should have clarified how many puffs of the inhaler I was taking each time I was using it.

Carrying the tag of being the first player to fail a drugs test was bad enough, but the fact that it was due to the asthma, which I'd worked so hard to overcome as a young footballer … the irony wasn't lost on me, put it that way.

When the whole thing was resolved I was flooded with messages from people who had asthma themselves – county players, club players and even kids who wanted to overcome the condition in order to play a sport they had a passion for. So in that sense, a lot of positivity came out of it.

Looking back at the whole thing now, I remember feeling as though the carpet had been pulled from under me. I think the entire matter was handled extremely poorly, and the leaking of my name to the press I still find frustrating and upsetting.

I couldn't comprehend that there were GAA officials on the International Rules tour – officials I would have been in contact with throughout the trip – who, when I stood in front of them at the hearing, addressed me as if I was a stranger.

What I had learned from the Donncha O'Connor incident probably helped me cope with this situation, but the one area I struggled with was the effect I thought it was having on my family. I was constantly picturing my parents going to Mass in the local church or shopping in the village and hearing that their son had failed a drugs test – before I'd had a chance to tell them the story. People are always going to speculate, and that speculation tends to incline towards the harsh end of the spectrum.

People have asked me since why I didn't come out at the time with a statement or a comment, but it was a minefield that I didn't want to get involved in. In the end I was vindicated, but it wasn't easy to be silent from November to February while plenty of people were happy to talk about my future.

In my first years with the Kerry senior team, I felt unstoppable: I won an All-Ireland medal in my debut year and bounced back from defeats to achieve more success, but the diving incident and the failed drugs test were personal. They drained me. Even now, going back in detail over both makes me feel uneasy.

But one thing I must highlight is the support I got and the advice I was given throughout the years from those who know me best.

The support of my own family, Rathmore GAA club and Kerry GAA was never in question. I can't thank them enough for that, at a time when so many stayed clear. As a result of the failed drug test and subsequent hearings, I'd estimate Kerry GAA were €30,000 out of pocket, but this figure, or the sheer hassle involved throughout the whole process, was never mentioned by those who helped me along the way.

From the Kerry county board chairman Jerome Conway to my own club chairman Andy McCarthy, the focus was on getting my name cleared, and everything else came second.

The only way I could pay everyone back was on the pitch.

I didn't speak about this when it happened, and the loneliness of the situation probably crept up on me.

I was confident my name would be cleared, but it was constantly in the media and a lot of people in the media and on social media – and on nights out – were obviously happy to draw their own conclusions and to share their own opinions in controversial and misleading headlines.

At the time I felt embarrassed that I was an asthmatic, something I'd had to fight with all my life in order to get where I was in my career. I didn't chose asthma, it chose me, and I was explaining myself with a cloud hanging over my head.

It drained me, as it dragged on for nearly six months, and that spilt into my work and my personal life. Although I knew I would be cleared, it wasn't an easy time. And though it made me stronger in the long run, it was another blow I didn't need.

12

Walking Away

Getting back to football after the drugs test controversy, my head wasn't right. I can see that now
with the benefit of hindsight. I was caught between
wanting to repay those who had supported me and a
stark realisation: I wasn't enjoying football any more.

Internally the energy and motivation weren't there; my
focus was on looking externally for a way out. Because
of that, everyone and everything else were to blame if
things didn't go as planned. And so I stumbled into 2009,
my preparation sidetracked, playing catch-up in terms of
fitness, sharpness and game time.

When we lost the Munster final to Cork that year it
was clear there were going to be changes. Jack brought
Mike McCarthy back into the camp – a Rolls-Royce of a
player, he came in at centre-back for me and reinvigorated
the whole team.

It was a master stroke from Jack. Great for the team and great for Mike McCarthy, to come back like he did and make such an impact – as only a player and a man like Mike could do.

Back then I was thinking differently. It was the first time I'd been dropped, and in terms of selection the first real setback I'd had to deal with.

After turning the Munster final defeat to Cork around and getting through a few close battles in the qualifiers, we went on to win the All-Ireland that year.

It was a season of ups and downs. On one side, I was surrounded by energy and inspiration.

Paul Galvin was a man on a mission and rightly went on to win player of the year, Darran O'Sullivan lifted the Sam Maguire as captain, Mike McCarthy enjoyed a brilliant comeback, and the team produced some huge performances, including in the All-Ireland quarter-final against Dublin.

However, I wasn't feeding off all of these positives. Instead I found the year draining, and if I'm being honest, I was probably sucking energy out of the camp – a negative person to be around. In short, I didn't know who I was. I'd lost my love for a sport that had given me so much life, and I'd become a different person, and that didn't change as we headed into the 2010 season.

Should I have acted sooner? Maybe.

Nowadays I would have no problem speaking out, asking a manager for a chat or even getting professional help, but I didn't see that as an option back then.

Some of that related to my persona, or how I perceived my own persona – as a player I played on the line, but outside of football I kept to myself.

From the outside I probably looked like someone who was very deep in himself, and I wouldn't blame other players for leaving me alone when that was the message I was giving off.

The league went well for me in 2010, and I could sense people's opinions changing: 'He's back to himself now and he'll be a big addition to the team this year.'

However, I wasn't enjoying it at all. The gloss was gone from the whole experience, and I was just going to training after work for the sake of it – there was no enjoyment in it.

And that lack of enjoyment can come out in different ways. I got sent off in the last league game against Tyrone, out of frustration more than anything else. The following week we played with our clubs and I knew after that game I had reached breaking point. I felt drained and knew my mind was in a bad place. I went socialising with my club-mates and I sent a text to a friend who I knew would run with the story:

I'm pulling the plug on my GAA career.

After that we had a week's training camp in Portugal to get us prepared for the championship.

On the morning we were due to fly out, I texted Jack to say I wouldn't be going, then switched off the phone.

That was very different to the person I used to be. I'd always loved those training weeks, and missing them wasn't an option, in my mind. I used to live for the intensity of the camp and training hard for the week.

I was conscious of my team-mates, management and support staff, not to mention the resources invested by the county board in funding those camps. Showing that much disrespect was something I could never have imagined: I was never selfish and I knew this was completely out of character.

After my no-show, rumours weren't long springing up, as usual. I hadn't gone on the training camp. I was meeting Jack for talks. I wasn't meeting Jack for talks. Eventually it was released: I'd walked away for personal reasons.

In truth, my battle was different at that time. I'd walked away from something I loved, something that had given me an identity, and I was getting caught up in the after-effects of stepping away. I was over-thinking everything, looking further down the line, wondering how my situation might get better.

It took a while for me to realise I needed help – and that was the by-product of close family and friends noticing something was up. Noticing that something needed to be done. On their advice, I went to the Aiséirí centre for six weeks of therapy. It's a residential treatment centre for adults, where you stay on site for an agreed period, focusing solely on your recovery.

For me it was one of the bravest steps I ever took.

You can talk about running out in front of a packed Croke Park, but for me stepping out of the car that day and walking in through the doors of the centre was like nothing I had ever experienced. Even now I can't pinpoint exactly what it was. Nerves? Anxiety? Being completely overwhelmed? Maybe all of the above.

I couldn't speak highly enough of the staff there. Any uncertainty I had walking in was soon squashed.

There's no contact with the outside world – one of the reasons I chose to go there in the first place – no phones, no social media. It's just about you and getting yourself right.

Before that I'd found that kind of relaxation impossible – there was always something that kept my mind going at 100 miles an hour: a problem, an issue … something.

As a result of that overactive mind I was totally drained, both physically and mentally. It was an accumulation, a build-up of all those years of driving myself, getting knocked back and seeing no way out.

Relaxing had become very difficult. Even something like going out for a few drinks with the lads after a game wasn't fun because my mind was so negative.

I was someone who kept things to himself, who let those negative feelings fester rather than taking the opportunity to talk them through.

It probably boiled right down to who I was at that stage of my life. That was the way I grew up and dealt with things – or didn't deal with them, to be more accurate.

Throughout the whole process, from realising I needed help to leaving the centre, there were numerous times when I'd question how I could face a particular situation.

I remember specifically standing at the door of my inspector's office, about to tell him that I needed some time off, that my mind wasn't in a great place and that I needed some professional help.

I was very lucky that the gardaí were so supportive of me. What I thought was going to be a challenge soon turned into a discussion about how they could get me the help I needed.

At the end of your time in Aiséirí you have a little ceremony where you burn all the thoughts and feelings you dealt with over the course of your six weeks there.

That's a very hard feeling to describe because it's wrapped up in the entire experience of being in the centre, but the memory makes me smile every time.

A weight was lifted. Everything I had been holding onto for years had been released.

I've made plenty of mistakes in my life and I'm sure I'll make plenty more, but accepting that made a big difference to me. So did hearing something as simple as 'Mistakes are a normal part of life'.

Instead of sinking into dark days and thinking negative thoughts about myself and worrying about the future, I changed.

I became a more open person and saw myself differently. I realised that my GAA career wasn't everything. I wore a jersey, fair enough, but that was just one chapter in my life.

After all that had happened – the diving incident, the failed drugs test, being dropped – a negativity had crept in to my thinking and I went into a slump.

The asthma fed into that, too, because with attacks I'd have a sense of *Why me? Why this?* And to be honest, the social media side of things didn't help either. I was in the habit of looking at things like supporter forums, and when I did, there might be 10 comments about me in a game. Nine could be quite positive but if one person said something negative, that's the one I'd take on board and mull over.

I was drained. I wasn't enjoying life and I could have walked away from everything that was good. I realise now that I might have come across as unapproachable, or as someone who wouldn't take advice on board even if it was offered.

The benefit of Aiséirí, though, was that I dealt with things rather than let them fester inside. Before that I didn't have the ability to do that: even if I went out socialising I would get emotional after a couple of drinks as all the built-up feelings came out. But Aiséirí taught me that life is for living, not holding all of these issues inside.

Stepping away from the real world was the key. Going into Aiséirí, part of me was thinking, *What are people going to make of me doing this?* But that was my problem all along – worrying about what people were thinking. That's what was draining me.

When I came out, though, I could face problems head-on, I could discuss issues. I'm not perfect, by any means, but the experience there taught me to enjoy life. Things will happen, but now when they do, I deal with them.

Was I depressed? I think everyone goes through tough times, and for me that period was rock bottom. Everything feeding in was negative, and I needed an intervention. The years of allowing things to build up and not letting them out ... it all came to a head.

The gloss was gone off everything, and I was questioning myself on the most basic elements of my sporting identity – why had I got into Gaelic football in the first place, and wouldn't I have been better off if I'd never played at all?

I wasn't supposed to train for the six weeks I was in Aiséirí but, of course, I found a field that I could run around, and three or four times a day, six days a week, I hit that field. Sometimes I sprinted and other days I jogged.

There was no marking out of distances, no recoding times; I didn't have any goal. It was purely for the release and I think there's a lot to be learned from that.

Sometimes we get caught up in hitting targets, numbers, worrying about where we should be, instead of just getting out there and enjoying the feeling of getting it done.

Those sessions helped me through those few weeks and helped to re-instil in me the love of exercise.

It was a welcome distraction, taking my mind away also from wondering how Kerry were getting on in their first championship games against Tipperary and Cork.

When I left Aiséirí I went to see my parents, and there were lots of tears shed. They saw the change in me after my spell away. I was happier and more content.

My brother Kieran picked up on that in particular. He's been involved with nearly every Rathmore team I've played for over the years, and he's been an amazing driving force for me. I'm close to all my family, but in terms of sport I'm particularly close to Kieran, and he's always been there for me.

I'd done something that many people don't do, or can't do, and I felt all the better for it. Like everybody else, I have good days and bad days, but that experience helped me and made me the person I am today.

I went in to the centre as a negative, introverted, closed person with all the worries in the world on my shoulders, but I came out seeing things in a different light.

As simple as it sounds, that change came from talking. I couldn't see everything I had going for me. I couldn't see the support I had around me. All I needed was that refocus and talking aloud.

My apprehension about going to therapy probably stemmed from a fear that people would think less of me – which itself probably links back to a belief that I should act a certain way.

But having done it, I feel more respect for myself.

I knew it was a big step to take. I knew people were going to jump to their own conclusions. That feeling was borne out when I met some of those people later, and they said they'd heard various stories about me.

It's good that people these days feel freer to talk about the challenges of mental health, the fact that it's okay not to be okay.

I wasn't okay. I was looking for answers and couldn't find them.

Football has been fantastic to me, absolutely, but it's also a very selfish pastime. It has to be if you're at the top level: you're completely focused on your preparation, your fitness – on everything in terms of how it impacts on your game.

I dealt very badly with All-Ireland final defeats in 2005 and 2008, for example: it was like there was no tomorrow. I had to change that in myself and to find a balance. If I go for a run now I'll set myself a target, a time I have to beat, and I'll do my best to reach that target – but if I don't, it's no big deal.

Sometimes in life we carry the weight of the world on our shoulders, but thinking it will all be fine, it will all blow over. But inevitably it doesn't leave you, it keeps eating away at you, and all of a sudden you don't know the person looking back at you in the mirror.

Or you spend a career on the pitch being invincible, acting like nothing would faze you, but all the time something is bothering you and it's not being addressed. The lesson that 'it's okay not to be okay' was one I learned the hard way, and before I went into Aiséirí I was thinking I might develop a stigma because of admitting I needed help, but I came out with so much weight lifted from my shoulders and my mind in such a positive place.

If you need help, then get help. The lessons don't get any simpler than that. I returned to the playing field and 'Fallen idol' was the caption the following week. That wouldn't define me.

13

Denise

I met Denise in 2010.

At the end of that year, I was at a charity function in Killarney and we got chatting.

I fell for her very soon after we met as she was everything I was looking for in a life companion. She had been working in the Middle East just before we met but had come home to look after her mom, Mairead, who fell ill in late 2010. Mairead was originally from near my home place, Gneeveguilla, and she loved GAA. Mairead and I developed an instant bond and we had many meaningful conversations. She was a very interesting and well-read lady. She had so many unique characteristics and anyone who knew her loved her positivity, creativity and humour. I responded to Denise and her family so well because they are extremely open, welcoming and friendly people. As a result of the change in myself and my mindset, I found it so easy to relate to and form unique relationships with each of them when I got to know them.

Denise has many traits that I appreciate and value. She loves to travel and I felt like she opened the whole world up to me in that sense. She studied and worked abroad for a few years and has great friends dotted around the globe. She also had the attitude that we could get to places even if we were busy. For instance, if Kerry had a training camp, after it we'd have a couple of weeks off before getting into championship training – so we would head off to Mexico for a few weeks, the Middle East and around Europe – something I'd never have even considered possible previously while committed to football. This opened up a very exciting chapter in my life. Denise was also big into her fitness and so many of our trips were devoted to intense training together and relaxing from busy working lives.

In December 2011 her mom sadly passed away. It was such a tough time for Denise and her two sisters, Sinead and Moira, as they had the most loving, supportive and irreplaceable relationship with their mom. They all pulled together, and we got into the habit of going abroad for a number of the Christmases that followed: ourselves, Moira and Sinead and their husbands, Nik and Damian. We made some precious and unforgettable memories during those winter trips. They were like journeys we made in Mairead's memory. It's a raw time to lose someone, the week before Christmas, so the change of scenery each time we went away was welcome. The time I'd spent with Mairead, getting to know her, strengthened my bond with Denise. Their incredible relationship and love would have been difficult to comprehend if I hadn't seen it first-hand. Denise to this day mentions that her mom shaped her into the person she is and taught her about the most important aspects of life.

I proposed in Dubai in 2012 and she said yes, thankfully! We got married in the Algarve in August 2015 and our celebrations took place at the Pine Cliffs Resort. It was a two-week holiday for our close family, and the memories we made at that time are unforgettable.

It was also the height of the football season. Kerry had beaten Kildare and were through to an All-Ireland semi-final against Tyrone. I approached Éamonn Fitzmaurice and Cian O'Neill because there was a three-week gap to the Tyrone game, and I asked them for a programme I could follow during my two weeks in the Algarve. Between my brother Kieran and Denise and her sisters, I had a training partner every morning, sometimes at 5 a.m., just before sunrise. I trained hard every day, in different parts of Villamoura and around the Algarve. It was very rewarding in the beautiful surroundings and gorgeous sunshine.

The training programme I followed was no problem to Denise. Athletics, basketball and Gaelic football were her sports of choice growing up. She was reared with an understanding of sport and what's needed to succeed. She travelled the country with athletics and won a number of gold All-Ireland athletic medals for sprints and long distance. On my initial trips to her house I saw plenty of medals on show that she and her sister Moira had won: I knew then that they were serious about their sporting commitment. That interest in health and fitness was a bond between us too.

She's educated, motivated and enthusiastic about life. I might as well admit that she has a better sense of style than me too and she certainly advised me and improved me on that score.

I had a changed mentality some time before I met Denise in 2010. Football wasn't the be-all and end-all for me any more. Before 2010 I found it hard to realise that football had a place in my life but so did other things and Denise was a big help in how I learned to manage that, because I could talk to her about those issues and she understood where I was coming from. She was very understanding and good at unpacking my thoughts, advising on coping mechanisms and encouraging my competitive edge. I guess being a GAA player can be very self-centred and I was conscious of all the events that Denise had to attend solo, from friends' engagements to birthdays and weddings. I was her plus one but couldn't be present so many times. I still continue to thank her for her patience, acceptance and understanding of my commitments.

She was there for all the injuries, all the strains, all the aches. Denise had her own interests and pathway during the football turmoil, which was always refreshing and distracting for me. For example, we rarely spoke about football, which was an amazing aspect of our relationship.

About three months before we got married I was playing for Kerry in a challenge against Limerick in Austin Stack Park. At one stage I had a shuffle with the player I was marking and he swung back his elbow. He wiped my nose across my face, which wasn't a great look for any prospective groom. I was brought down to the hospital by Niall 'Botty' O'Callaghan and I requested a doctor I knew: when he came in I explained that I was getting married three months later and was concerned about the aesthetics of my nose for my wedding day. He instantly broke my nose back into place for me. My memory of that episode is Niall covering his eyes in the corner of the room while the doctor broke the bone back in. I warned Niall not to say anything to Denise.

I got to bed late that night and thought it best to leave things slide – until the physio at the time, Eddie Harnett, rang Denise the same night asking if I was alright. Denise asked him why I wouldn't be alright. Caught!

Meeting Denise taught me that there was a world outside the GAA and that there was so much more to experience and moments to live for.

If you're involved in sport it can be very self-centred. There are great aspects to being in that bubble but I hadn't realised there were other aspects of life that were just as enjoyable, if not more so.

Denise introduced me to the world that goes on outside that bubble. We're also blessed with our two daughters, Lucia and Lilah, which is a series of life lessons of a whole different order!

14

All for the Club

Playing through the Pain

In any changing room, you always hear coaches and players talk about putting down a marker early in a big game. Our big game in 2011 was the club championship final, in Fitzgerald stadium, Rathmore versus Laune Rangers. A chance to win a first senior county trophy in 12 years.

I'm not one for speaking in the dressing room, but more than in any other game I felt a responsibility to lead. It had been so long since our last senior title, and the club deserved it – this team deserved it.

This club final was four weeks after our All-Ireland final loss to Dublin, so it was a welcome distraction, but that was another reason to believe nothing but winning was acceptable.

It was a typical October day, mist covering the McGillycuddy Reeks in the background, the rain starting to teem down, conditions underfoot slippery.

The game went to and fro but after less than 10 minutes of the first half a ball broke out under the stand sideline: it was a 50/50 ball, with myself and Peter Crowley (a team-mate with Kerry, now an opponent) going after it in a full-blooded collision. We bounced off each other and there was an almighty crack, but in the collision his knee caught me just below my own kneecap.

I got straight up and attempted to jog back into position but before I knew it I was down on the floor again.

The pain was severe: the adrenaline kicked in, but it soon wore off and the pain wasn't easing.

Dan O'Sullivan, our physio, ran on and I asked him to strap it up to get me to half-time. What was the sight of me limping off after a hit going to do to the morale of the team, after all?

I was playing midfield, so up until half-time I stationed myself in the full-forward line.

My focus was purely on the next ball. In my head I felt if I could win a ball near the D and pop it off, it would bring something to the team: it had to be better than sitting up in the stand watching on.

I was trying to out-think the full-back I was now marking. What did I hate defending against? How could I gain an advantage?

I won the first ball kicked in, fielding the ball at the top of the D, landing ready to get my shot off. With my left leg strapped I thought the defender would cover my right – so I used my injured leg, driving my foot through the ball. Point.

The pain was unbearable, shooting up through the foot, but on the bright side it put some uncertainty in the full-back's mind. He wasn't going to hare up the field and leave me limping around if I could pick off scores, so he stayed back.

Soon after it got even better. Mike O'Riordan won a great ball for us and came in along the endline, and when the Laune Rangers lads went to take him I was thinking, *Here we go, fairytale stuff – he'll dink it in to me for a goal.* But he was pulled down for a free.

I got another point soon after. I turned in to my man when I got the ball because I always hated a forward doing that to me. I burrowed through and got a shot off with my right.

I wasn't moving much from the D but the threat was there at least, something for them to worry about.

At half-time I had to walk the length of the pitch back to the dressing room stand located behind the opposite goalpost.

The pain was still severe, but my mind was made up: I wasn't going off. With each step I was getting more wound up by the possibility that I mightn't be coming out for the second half, so when I got to the dressing room Dan got me up on the table to have a further inspection.

'How bad is it?' he asked me.

'Pretty bad,' I said.

He took off the strapping and moved his hand up the leg.

'I think that's the fibula head there,' he said, pointing to the bone sticking out below my kneecap.

He started to push it back in – I can feel the pain when I talk about it now. It still leaves a sickening taste, but at the time I asked Dan to strap the area up and I'd see how things went in the second half.

The instructions were clear at half-time. I couldn't move, so the lads were to drop it in around the square and I'd see what I could do.

With the fibula pushed back in and strapped, I bit my lip and headed back out onto the field.

Fifty minutes in, my race was run. After clear instruction to put it into the square, Tom O'Sullivan came flying up the wing, pinging a 40-yard crossfield ball out to the opposite sideline. But when I tried to get across to it, that was it. I'd pushed the broken bone as far as it could go.

The game went down to the wire, but we eventually got over the line by two points.

We'd been senior for 12 years without winning a title, but at the final whistle Rathmore lads were dropping to their knees with the pure emotion of the win – and exhaustion, after being under siege for the last 10 minutes.

I thought of Weeshie Fogarty and his way of saying in commentary for those kinds of games that you could look over at the scoreboard and out at the McGillycuddy Reeks, and the emotion of that sank in.

So did the emotion of seeing my neighbour, Kieran Cahill, go up and accept the cup. It was an amazing feeling, and it marked a turning point for us as a club as well – we'd been senior for years without winning any silverware, even though we were beating the biggest names in Kerry club football. It blended the group, young and old; it showed us what we were capable of. It went deep.

Adrenaline keeps you going in a game like that because it's about getting over the line, but where injuries are concerned, that can only take you so far.

I've read a few papers on that type of injury since. I think it was Dr Con Murphy who gave a full analysis on the possibilities of playing on with a broken fibula but only if the break is located at the ankle or side of the shin: mine was a break of the fibula head.

I've had injuries before, from breaking noses to accidentally getting a boot in the face before the 2006 All-Ireland final. But this injury was different: it was more psychological than physical. The pain was there, but taking a breath, looking down and pushing a bone back into place brings different challenges. If it was the beginning of my football career I'm not sure I would have had the resilience to do what I did. I honestly think that that capability was born out of having had the ups and downs in the preceding years.

We had lost the 2011 All-Ireland final four weeks before, but I'd bounced back to win man of the match in the club semi-final. And when I was sitting on a physio bench at half-time in the final, about to make a call on whether I should continue, my feelings were clear: enough was enough, no more excuses. I'll lead this young team. It's my club, my responsibility.

That day definitely changed me as well as my club.

The celebrations put it all into perspective.

We returned home on the team bus, back across Barraduff Bridge and pass Lisnagrave Cross and the number of people who came out to greet us was unreal. Then up to my own place in Mounthorgan, and more people, more bonfires, and into the Old Chapel Bar.

Dermie Moynihan, who's been with the club ever since I was a child, came up trumps just as I got off the bus at Rathmore: he had a pair of crutches waiting for me and it was like Our Lord giving me a spare pair of legs.

We went into the local for a drink – all your friends, your club-mates, the whole community, the reason you push for wins like this.

There was another factor as well. When I came back to football after walking away from Kerry, it was these people, my club, who welcomed me back, and I was keen to repay the faith they'd shown in me.

The night finished off and the pain was getting severe – not helped, of course, by being jammed into a bar for the evening where there were people walking on my foot and banging into me.

The following morning I got on to Mike Finnerty, the Kerry doctor, and he organised an X-ray for me in Tralee.

I was driving back through Killarney when some of the lads rang and asked where I was – they were going around the schools with the cup; at this point it was killing me to work the clutch in the car with my foot, the pain was so bad, so I told them to work away without me.

In the hospital a doctor came out to take my details before the X-ray. 'How did you hurt your leg?' he asked. 'Was it work-related?'

'Ah no,' I said. 'Football.'

He looked at his watch: it was still morning on a Monday, so obviously he was wondering.

'Was it today?'

'No, we had a game yesterday.'

'Why didn't you come in after the game?'

'Well, I played on, and then we had a homecoming afterwards and I went to that.'

And he didn't speak to me again until later.

After the X-ray he told me to sit in a wheelchair.

'I'm grand,' I said.

'No, get into the wheelchair.'

He told me to ring someone to come and collect me. I rang Denise and by the time she got to the hospital I was in a cast from my toes to my hip: it was confirmed I'd broken the fibular head, a straight fracture across the bone.

'Because you played on, you'll be in plaster for six weeks,' said the doctor. 'Probably longer.'

The adrenaline had worn off by then and it was beginning to sink in. Because Rathmore were senior, there was a chance of representing the county in the Munster club championship, but I knew I'd miss that.

Denise brought me up to her sister Moira's house, and she had the pouffe out for me to put the leg on.

In the meantime I was getting messages from the other players: 'We're putting on the video of the game here in Cahill's, we're watching it.'

The emotion of the day, the injury, the win, the homecoming, then the visit to the hospital – the whole experience was coming together and catching up with me.

The celebrations went on for weeks, but one story still makes me smile.

After the game, I was on crutches chatting to the pals, feeling good about the win, though the pain was getting more severe.

One old lad with his friends came up to me: I'd clocked him looking at me for a while beforehand, and could see that he had something he wanted to get off his chest. He eventually made his move, coming over for a word.

'I'm after thinking about it all evening,' he said. 'Jesus, you could have cost us that match today.'

I burst out laughing. You just have to love that about the GAA.

Everyone knows their own body, and there's a balancing act between two things – what you know you're capable of physically and what bit of craziness you need to bring to a game.

The lesson I might have learned that day is how you can make a bad injury a hundred times worse, but I prefer to focus on the positive. The lesson I picked up from the homecoming in 2004, the importance of the club, fed into the need to repay the club for all the support they'd given me over the years. That's what made the difference that day in Killarney.

15

Losing Dad

My pre-season was tough enough in 2012 because I was recovering from the broken leg, but I'd rediscovered my appetite for football fully after walking away from the Kerry setup a couple of years before.

The flip side was that by then I was 32 years of age, but my attitude was that every year was a bonus, and my focus was on being an addition to what was inside in the Kerry camp.

Whether starting or not, it's important to bring some value to the setup. The last thing I would have wanted is for people to be able to say, 'Yeah, he was dropped again and now he's just a major downer to have around the place.' As part of that, I was practically living in the gym to rehab my leg. I went in to John Sugrue, the physio in Killarney, after the cast was taken off and he asked me where the crutches and the special boot were.

'I left them out in the boot of the car,' I said.

'I won't be treating you unless you're on the crutches and in the boot,' he said.

It's amazing – you think you're doing the best work you can to get back but you might be doing more damage: I wasn't long getting those items out of the boot of the car and playing by the rules.

I missed the first couple of league games in 2012. Alan O'Sullivan was training Kerry then, and the sessions were tough, but so enjoyable.

I can remember Daniel Bohane of Austin Stacks being injured as well, and we were doing a lot of tackle-bag work together in Kerins O'Rahilly's pitch in January and February in an effort to recover and remain in the game, both of us longing to get back to playing football: the appeal of hammering into a tackle bag doesn't last too long.

The year built and built, and my goal was the same as always – to start in the championship. But I had a new position: full-back.

I enjoyed playing there. It's one of those places on the field where there's always a buzz when the ball lands in there, but there's also an old-fashioned element to playing there which hasn't changed down the years: the duel between two players.

Some guys might think I'm crazy, but no matter what happens in a game it's a special situation when the full-back is one-on-one with a forward. They can go left or right, and you're the only one between them and a goal … I enjoyed that element of the position – the challenge, the responsibility and the unpredictability.

It's an unforgiving place too. If you're not absolutely tuned into what you're doing it can get very embarrassing very fast, but I enjoyed that level of pressure as well.

And there's a physical aspect to it too. That season isn't too long ago but even then there would have been plenty of teams who, if the situation demanded, would just try to hit the full-forward line with a 60/40 ball: we did it ourselves many times in games.

My first big test on the edge of the square was probably that year's Munster final against Cork, when I picked up Nicholas Murphy.

He suited me in that he's a big man, six foot five, but he had a pair of hands that the ball would glue to and I was relishing the new challenge.

Nowadays the buzzword is 'systems', but then it was 'containing' – you had to contain your man, and Jack was very strong on that approach, to go out and contain your man, end of story.

For a defender, that's good because you know your job and it's straightforward. Was that selfish? No, because it was man on man, and if your man was getting the better of you, someone else came in to have a go at quieting him instead of you. That was very much in line with how we'd learned our football the first day as backs, to block out the opposing forward.

Of course that's easier said than done. For a forward like Nicholas, all he needed to do was win one ball and give it off to someone for a goal and his job was done for the day: he didn't even need to get on the scoreboard if he was setting up scores for other players, so keeping him scoreless wasn't the only task at hand.

People would often ask me, 'How would you approach marking this player or that player?'

The ultimate balancing act is being fully aware that your man doesn't need to score if he can set up others. And to stop him doing that, the best way is to beat him to the ball in the first place and dictate the play.

We got over Cork and faced Donegal in the All-Ireland quarter-final. There was massive hype and a real buzz about this one because the rumours were floating out of Donegal about the training they were doing, the tactics, Jim McGuinness's influence on them. The whole pre-battle was intriguing to all stakeholders.

For me the focus was Michael Murphy. I'd picked him up in a league game above in Ballyshannon. I remember 40 yards of space in front of us and McGuinness telling his players – roaring at them – to leave it into Michael. So I knew the challenge I faced.

He's a top-class player, he's physically powerful, but not everyone appreciates his thinking, his reading and comprehension of the game. He's a step or two ahead of everyone else on the field, he knows what he wants to do with the ball before he gets it, and he always chooses the right option.

I would class him as one of the most unselfish players I've ever marked. In the quarter-final he was going out the field and then coming back in around the square, which posed all sorts of challenges, which I loved. Years of playing centre-field with the club meant I was comfortable under a dropping ball, even with a good fielder against me. The mantra was simple: break the ball away from him all the time and rely on the other lads to pick up the breaks.

Still, the game turned on a little bit of unpredictability: Colm McFadden took a sideline kick in the first half and myself and Murphy were jostling and shoving underneath the ball as it dropped in, but it took a bounce and shot into the top corner of the net without either of us touching it.

The two of us were left looking at each other – *What happened there?* – but in every big game a team needs a little bit of luck to win it, and that was their slice.

We had chances late on but they held out. Karl Lacey was excellent for Donegal that day and popped up with the insurance point for them, but it was the kind of game you look back on and think of all the possible scenarios. I always say you don't look back on the medals, but you do look back on the memories, the what-ifs, the might-have-beens.

As a player the basic question is 'Did I do everything I could have?' In one sense there's always more that can be done, and that year we were left wondering about the one that got away, maybe.

That's not to say we'd have won the All-Ireland necessarily – that was just the quarter-final, after all – but it was Jack's last day in office, and there was a sense of the end of an era about that game.

Losing had one upside. I hadn't been to an All-Ireland final as a spectator ever, believe it or not, so Denise and I made a weekend of it and attended the game, experiencing all the hype first-hand for the first time.

The Kerry county board provided a couple of tickets. I'd known Alan Smullen for years, the manager of the Croke Park hotel and a very good friend, so I asked him if there was any room availability, to be in the centre of the chaos. It was cheeky of me to request a room, with Mayo and Donegal descending in their thousands on Dublin, but as always he looked after us.

It was a fantastic experience to just be around Dublin for a few days that weekend, soaking up the atmosphere without any pressure. Walking around the city, feeling the build-up, hitting the shops and the clubs at night.

There was evidence of the All-Ireland everywhere we went, but for me it was hugely enjoyable because there was no sense of the pressure which comes with a game. (Although when we ducked into Kehoes for a drink I noticed a row of football referees at the counter having a drink, obviously making a weekend of it themselves. I was the target of their banter so after a swift drink I said to Denise we'd leave them to their own company.)

It showed me a whole other side of the GAA experience, the way you could enjoy the weekend and look forward to a game you had no stake in. The whole weekend I had Denise driven crazy, saying things like, 'So this is what it's like out on a Saturday of an All-Ireland – isn't it so much fun and an absolute great buzz.'

We met up with friends; we dropped into The Boar's Head to meet Hugh Hourican, a massive GAA figure who every player in the country knows and respects, and there were players there of all generations – I'm talking about guys I grew up watching – and it was a pleasure being introduced to them, chatting, laughing and conversing about all things GAA.

Then on the Sunday morning at breakfast, the Mayo and Donegal people were asking who'd win, the crowds, the excitement – it was just an electric atmosphere and I loved every minute of it. It was an eye-opener for me, a glimpse of life outside the four white lines.

But I could also see how the experience was a bit different for those spectators with something on the line, from the people with a family member playing to the supporters who were just anxious about the outcome.

The last time I'd been in Croke Park for a game, outside of being a player, had been back in 1996 for the Kerry–Mayo semi-final. We took our seats, and as I was looking down at the two teams waiting to meet the president I was a little taken aback, thinking, *Was I down there last year?* It didn't seem real at all, though I also knew how the players felt, the rush of adrenaline, the sense of anticipation.

People can probably remember that Donegal won that day, and that Michael Murphy got a stormer of a goal. I was delighted for him – he deserved his day in the sun. My heart went out to the Mayo players and supporters, naturally enough. I remember going out onto Jones's Road afterwards, seeing the slump in the Mayo people's shoulders as they walked along.

As we strolled through the streets of Dublin to the train station, the chat was still rolling on, people dissecting the game, the back and forth, strangers connecting with a common interest.

My phone rang when I was on the train: my dad. He had huge admiration for Michael Murphy and for the way a player like him not only played on a big day, but really performed when that was needed, that he didn't let anything affect him.

We had the usual chat: Dad asked where I was sitting in Croke Park, what did I think of Michael Murphy's goal – his admiration couldn't have been more genuine if I'd scored the goal myself.

He was the same about Aidan O'Shea, saying he'd love to see him win an All-Ireland some day in the future, and at the end I was wondering was he happy to see Donegal win or was he sad to see Mayo lose. He just loved to talk about the games.

I worked the following day up in Cork district court, and there was still an afterglow from the match and what had been a fabulous weekend.

I was thinking that when you lose a final, the very last place you'd want to be the next day is work – sometimes players are – but that was irrelevant to me this time. People were chatting about the game all day, and it was so enjoyable to talk about it myself as a neutral.

Home to Faha, where we lived at the time, and that Monday night Denise and myself went into Killarney to meet friends of hers home from Dublin. It was a quiet night and I was back home early ahead of another day's work in Cork.

My phone rang at around 4 a.m., with HOME coming up on it, but that wasn't uncommon.

My first thought was, *The alarm at home in Rathmore is going off again,* because that house alarm was hooked up to our phones, my brothers' and sisters', and my parents were devils to turn on the alarm, go to bed and maybe set it off randomly.

With one of those calls, though, when I would answer you would get an automated voice – *The alarm is going off* – with a beeping sound in the background.

But this time there was no beeping. It was Kieran, my brother: 'Aidan, you need to come home.'

'What do you mean?' I said.

'There's something wrong with Dad.'

Denise woke up immediately and asked what was the matter. I told her what Kieran had said and then I asked him what was wrong.

'I think he's passed away,' he said.

Anyone who's been through a similar experience will know the feeling. You have to gather yourself together and drive home – a drive you've done hundreds of times without thinking, but this time it seems to take an eternity.

Through Killarney, up through Shrone Cross, and persuading yourself all the way: *This isn't real at all. I'll get to the top of the hill here and it won't be real.*

When I got to the top of the hill I could see the ambulance parked outside the house. Then it began to sink in.

As a garda I'd often be called out to a sudden death, and it's a tough job. You're going out to a family who've lost someone, and whether the deceased is young or old it's very hard for the family to take that on board. And seeing someone come in with a uniform on, to take details of the person who's gone … you need to be very sensitive doing that. The same if you call to someone's door to tell them they've lost a member of the family. And now I had to walk into my own house, into the same situation.

I pulled in and went in the front door. On the left going in there's a glass door into the sitting room where my dad used to sit. A little couch facing the TV, with videos of games stacked everywhere, the remote control close at hand: that was his spot.

But if I came in, he'd always pause the game he had playing on TV because he knew that I hated watching old games.

Looking in through the glass door that night, though? No sign of him.

I went into the next room. Kieran and my mom were there, and my dad was lying in the bed. Mom said, 'Thade, Aidan's here now, wake up.'

It was beyond emotional. You want to keep yourself together for your mom, but there are a hundred things going through your mind.

My immediate thought was that our last conversation had been about the All-Ireland final.

I've often mentioned community and family, and Rathmore club and community were unbelievable at that time. We kept Dad in the house, and like the old days, we stayed up with him during the nights.

It was both a tough few days and a memorable few days. The Rathmore lads and the Kerry team showed amazing support, but guys I'd played against through the years also came from all over the country to pay their respects.

These were men I'd gone to battle with in the past and here they were when I was at my lowest, coming in to pay their respects and offer their support. People who know the GAA will know that that's what you'd expect, but it's still great to get that support at those low points in life.

Rathmore were playing Laune Rangers in the championship the day after the funeral, and I played the game. They gave us a bit of a beating but I remember coming out of the dressing room in Fitzgerald stadium after the game and walking onto the empty pitch on my own and saying to myself, *I'm going to get up those steps in the Hogan stand in Croke Park for you, Dad, before I finish up.*

I wouldn't be the type of person to make a big deal out of that sort of thing or to share it with other people, so I kept it to myself.

But it drove me. Anyone who's been through that kind of experience knows that things get more challenging when everything dies down after a few weeks, and people aren't calling in or ringing. Everyone moves on, but the rawness is still real.

My mom had lost her best friend, someone she'd spent 50 years with. We can all take the people we love for granted, and that showed me, certainly, that we should never do that.

I had a flashback to when I still lived at home, coming in from work and asking Mom where Dad was.

'He's in the sitting room.'

And out I'd go. He'd have the remote in his hand, watching a game on TV he'd probably seen 10 or 20 times before.

He'd know I'd be coming and the pause button would be pressed, but after I'd said hello or got my gear and headed back out, the door would hardly be closed behind me and the TV would be on again and the commentary running away in the background.

And he'd settle back and enjoy it. He was a soft, gentle and kind soul.

*

There were a few names being mentioned when Jack stepped down, possibles and probables as Kerry manager. Éamonn Fitzmaurice had been a selector with Jack and to me it was clear he'd be the manager. Obviously I'd played with him and knew him as a very good player, but he also had all the qualities, skills and expertise you need in a manager.

Even though he's a young guy, he has a great way with people; he'd obviously learned a huge amount from being involved with Jack, and he brought his own personality into the mix, which was clear as well.

The first time he rang me as Kerry manager I was in the gym in Fitzgerald stadium. Typical of Éamonn's kindness and concern, he asked me about my family and my mom. That's his way, and I don't think it's something a person can be taught: either they're built that way and that's how they behave, or they're not.

We eventually got into the nitty-gritty of football, and he said I'd had a good year at full-back. He didn't say straight out he wanted me back the following year, but he did say he thought I had more to give.

I agreed, and the conversation ended with me looking forward to 2013.

I made sure I gave everything for the season ahead. Every evening we trained, I was there a good hour early. I ate the gym up and loved it. Bed every night at nine. I was loving my discipline.

A few years ago I saw Brian Cody giving a presentation about successful players and teams doing everything to a T, and that was me in 2013.

The only downside is that everything becomes about you, the player.

I was a driven man that year, really staying in my own lane. I was never one for long speeches in the dressing room, and I wasn't going to start in 2013 by telling the Kerry panel about how I was driven to succeed by the death of my dad, but it was definitely on my mind that year that a part of me was doing it for him.

Because of the work and discipline I had a good league. I enjoyed the games and felt great: the benefits of everything being done to perfection.

Éamonn had come in with a simple but very effective motive. If a player was going well from the start of the McGrath Cup, a mini knockout in Munster, he'd get a jersey. There were two sides to that message: one, it told players that if they weren't back in January or February for early training and someone else was, and performed well, the latter would get the jersey.

Second, it told the team to get right back into the business side of the season straightaway.

In the championship we beat Waterford and Tipperary to make the Munster final. A big day, but for me it was more a stepping-stone to prove myself, and I was also hugely focused on winning to fill the void of the loss of my dad. It was becoming an obsession at that point, where I was nearly thinking, as I looked around the dressing room, *I don't mind if you get the jersey, just get me up the steps of the Hogan stand in September.*

But still, I was probably playing as well as I ever had in the run-up to that Munster final, and in training we had an A v. B game the week of the match. (We'd have joked over the years that you were better off on the B team because at least you had a target – making the A team – while if you played on the A team there was every chance you could play yourself off it.)

It was hammer and tongs in that A v. B game. The prize for a good performance was a starting spot against Cork in a Munster final in Killarney, 40,000 people watching on.

At 33 I knew there weren't too many of those occasions left, but I was enjoying that internal game, and the number 3 jersey felt more and more comfortable on me with every game I played in that position.

We were near enough to half-time when it happened. One of the lads drew on a ball and I put out my hand to get a block on it – and I got a stab of extreme pain in my left arm.

I went down in a heap and could hear a couple of the players saying, 'Oh no,' as they came over.

I looked down and saw that my elbow wasn't where it should have been – it had moved around to the other side of the arm.

Patrick O'Sullivan, our chairman and a great friend, said later that the roaring that came out from me was frightening. No surprise: my own first thought was, *That's career-ending, anyway.*

It's a cliché to say it felt like I was there for an eternity, but in this case it's not far off the truth. I got a couple of injections but they didn't take, so I couldn't move.

Meanwhile the lads were trying to continue to train. They ended up rolling in a set of portable goals and stationed it in front of me so they could salvage the session while I was in agony in the background.

The pain of the injury was one thing, but the pain of letting someone down – my dad – was far sharper. People might be surprised that I was even thinking of that in those circumstances, but I was. It was the only thing in my mind – that my career was over and I wouldn't make an All-Ireland final.

I can remember the ambulance pulling in and the driver hopping out: 'Have we a casualty?'

At that stage I'd had so much morphine I was making no sense. I know every roundabout and turn on the road between Killarney and Tralee and that journey seemed so long. I was talking to the nurse for the duration, but I haven't the foggiest idea what I was saying.

When I got to the hospital I can remember the doctor coming out, but that's it. I was knocked out then and they went to work.

I woke up and saw Denise. 'What happened?' I asked.

'They had a challenging job putting your elbow back in,' she said. 'They eventually got there.'

I'd dislocated my elbow and broken two bones there as well. The doctor came in and of course all I asked was how long would it take to heal. He said six to eight weeks for the fractures, a bad dislocation a few months … I had a cast on but my fingers were already beginning to swell up, despite the lightness of the cast.

I was trying to keep it together, but my emotions were high. Crying, thinking my football career was over, the motivation to win another All-Ireland in my dad's honour, my discipline, determination – all of those things were going through my mind.

Denise really understands sport herself, so she told me all the things I needed to hear: 'Look, you can't control the situation right now; we'll get you home soon and we'll re-evaluate your goals.' She was very good at keeping the situation as positive as possible.

Éamonn then arrived to visit, and one of the reasons I've so much respect for him is that he really cared for players. This man was under huge pressure – picking a team for his first Munster final in Killarney – but at that time he was really concerned for my well-being. 'We'll get you through this,' he said.

I turned on my phone and saw that the rumours were circulating about my football career being over.

I shouldn't have invested time in reading about it, but it got into my head, and I began to seriously consider that the rumours might have a grounding in fact.

When I got out of hospital I got a call from Ger Keane, who's one of the most positive people I've ever met. He's the Kerry physiotherapist and is excellent at his job, but beyond all of that his outlook was just what I needed: 'We'll get through this now, don't be worrying about it.'

I'd gone to him when I'd broken my leg and in some of the sessions I'd be gripping the chair, roaring, when he'd go at my leg, but he got me back quicker than anyone expected. His positivity rubbed off on me and I began to think there was a chance.

The cast was on in such a way that my hand was up by my shoulder – I couldn't bend the elbow, and fairly soon I got sick of people asking me if I'd regain full movement in the arm after the dislocation and fractures.

The Saturday night before the Munster final Éamonn rang me: 'We'd love you to be involved tomorrow, to come in to the game with us.' That was nearly the start of teams retaining players who were injured, keeping them involved, and I really appreciated it.

I met up with the players in the Aghadoe hotel. Mark Griffin, a block of a young guy, was starting at full-back and I made sure to encourage him. The two of us had battled for that jersey for years, and I was delighted for him; he was the right man coming in to play.

The focus of the players was amazing. Cork and Kerry in Killarney, of course the focus was there – but after Éamonn gave out the jerseys and the team meeting finished, he came over, shook my hand in front of the team and handed me a jersey too. Folded up neatly. A meaningful gesture.

I went on the bus with the rest, the jersey still folded in my hands. I opened it out on the bus. It was the number 3, with 'Munster Senior Football Final 2013' on the chest. A lovely touch by Éamonn, one that always sticks in my memory.

Kerry won, and it was a real Munster final experience. It was a hot day, the Reeks in the background, a buzzing crowd: the atmosphere was fantastic. We had a team meal afterwards and an enjoyable few drinks together.

The following day, though, my hand started swelling and was about four times the size it should have been. This was due to the position the hand was in and the cast, and as a consequence blood draining down into the hand.

I was still serious about getting back and was booked into the Sports Surgery Clinic in Santry for that Wednesday, so I went to Kerry training on Tuesday and said to Éamonn, 'Don't forget about me, I'll be running this week and getting the cast off.'

They were nodding at me when I said that – humouring me – but Kerry had drawn Cavan, with the game fixed for four weeks after the Munster final.

I knew that too. Winning the Munster final was of course the big thing, but I had another reason for wanting a Kerry victory.

In my last conversation with Ger Keane before that game I'd said, 'You know, if we win this weekend there'll be four weeks to the next game.'

And my mind started working. Was there a chance of

playing? He was talking about getting me to the clinic in Santry and I was wondering, *Could I get back?*

When I finished my appointment in Santry I was certain that the specialist was happy to see the back of me.

He'd say one thing to me and I'd agree, but in my mind I was focused on getting out on the field for the Cavan game, and I had the steps worked out: I'd have to play in the A versus B game the week of that game.

There was no talking to me. He listed out the injuries – fractures, a severe dislocation, some ligament damage, it'd take six weeks, or eight weeks to come back.

Was I taking any of that in? Not a word. My best counter-argument was that I was a quick healer – and I absolutely was – but I did ask if he'd cut off the cast in order to bring the swelling down, and he agreed to do that.

On the way home, I was going back and forth in my mind about the chance of getting back to play – optimistic one moment, down in the dumps the next. Someone would ring and I'd have the good side out – 'Yeah, yeah, very positive' – and then when I'd hang up I'd be fed up. Eyes brimming with tears.

I rang the two physios: Ger Keane when I arrived home, told him the cast was off and that I was ready to work, and then Eddie Harnett and again he was nothing but supportive and encouraging. I would play 'cat and mouse' with these two great men over the next few weeks in the quest to get back and they would not be found wanting either.

Ger was on summer holidays near Banna strand that time and I was off work, so I'd head to him every morning. On the first visit I was worried that the arm might never move the way it had, but his positivity, again, was huge.

He'd work on the arm and hand for maybe 45 minutes, get the swelling down, and then he'd tell me to rest up after a tough session.

'Grand,' I'd say, but rest was the last thing on my mind. I would hop in the car and sneak down onto the beach and do a tough running session, up and down the dunes.

Most of that sprinting was done with Denise, who put me through the paces.

We had trained in Banna beach with Kerry at one stage, and by going back to that spot and replicating the session, I knew I was getting great training done.

Then I'd go home, rest up and come back to Ger around five o'clock that same evening for another session of physio. If Kerry were training I'd head down to them then and maybe go to the gym or head out onto the front pitch with Pádraig Corcoran, one of the strength and conditioning coaches, and just run. Then back in to Eddie Harnett for physio, another man I couldn't praise highly enough.

Because of all that, I was getting fitter and fitter. I couldn't do anything with the hand so I wasn't getting any work done on my skills, but my fitness was excellent.

I'm quite sure everyone knew well that I was doing far more than I should have been – I'd get back to Ger's place in the evenings and he'd be saying, 'Did you rest up? You seem very tired,' after I'd put down an hour or two running up and down sand dunes on Banna.

The Thursday before the A v. B game I rang Éamonn and told him I was available.

'I don't know, Aidan, it's not four weeks since you got hurt,' he said.

'I know my own body,' I said. 'I'm up for it anyway and I want to play in the A versus B game.'

I togged out for it, and all of Ger Keane and Eddie Harnett's work had paid off. I must have had 90 per cent movement in the arm. I put down the fast healing to a combination of good genes and my own mindset at the time.

They sent Donaghy in on top of me and I was thinking, *The arm's going to be tested out here, anyway.*

Plenty of pulling and dragging. I got through the game and did well enough on Donaghy to make the panel for the Cavan game – number 25 or 26, but that didn't matter.

My attitude was that I had to get to the All-Ireland final in memory of my dad, although at the same time I truly felt I could help the team.

Cavan gave us enough of it in Croke Park but Kerry

got on top towards the end and I was wondering if I'd get a run out, but it wasn't to be.

I went out in Dublin that night with Denise. The following day my elbow was getting sore. At first I thought I might have banged it in the warm-up, but then my forehead started getting hotter and hotter. I ended up texting Ger Keane about it at around two on the Tuesday morning and when we went back to Kerry the following day the elbow was still totally inflamed.

I rang Dr Mike Moloney, the Kerry team doctor, and he said to come in for a look and that he'd book me in for a consultation in Cork later in the week. But in the meantime the elbow got worse. I couldn't train on the Tuesday. I told Éamonn something was wrong. Another manager could have said, 'Well, I told you so, what do you expect after coming back too soon.' But not him; that wouldn't be in his character. He was only concerned for my well-being.

I eventually went to Cork University Hospital, and when a doctor tried to take blood out of the elbow the fluid coming into the syringe was orange. There was an infection and I needed an operation in Santry.

Up to Santry then, and after the operation, I asked the surgeon when I'd be back playing. He didn't even answer, he just walked away from me.

Where my mind was, I saw that as a minor setback. Something I'd recover from. I was probably my own worst enemy, thinking I was invincible.

I was in Santry for three or four days before getting back home, but I didn't waste the time. I spent hours reading up on how to get the immune system back on track after an operation, so I loaded up on probiotics: my thinking was that I'd keep the immune system going until we were finished the season, and then I could crash again.

I went straight back into training with Kerry. At that stage I've no doubt the management were thinking that I was really pushing it, but I went out on the field, told Pádraig Corcoran that I was getting the stitches out in a day or two and that I was ready for running, according to the doctors.

'What doctor told you that?' he said.

'Well, I didn't get his name,' I said, 'but he said it was grand.'

After about 20 minutes of running I got the call from Pádraig. 'They're after ringing from Dublin, and they're afraid that infection has got into your bloodstream. Off the pitch with you.' They had looked at the results.

I was back training on the Thursday again anyway. The aim was to make the A versus B game – again – ahead of the All-Ireland semi-final against Dublin.

My arm was sore all the time; there's no point in saying otherwise. I was trying to move an elbow and arm that didn't want to move, so the physio sessions were torture, plain and simple. I was bending the legs of the table at times with the pain.

All of this time I was getting educated advice from Denise, telling me to relax, rest, recover, reassess and reset my goals. Of course, my stubborn self didn't accept her support.

When I got the mobility back in my arm, the punishment was worth it. Dublin in Croke Park, a full house in an All-Ireland semi-final. That was a massive incentive.

I made the panel, which was the first step. The team was going well, Gooch and Tomás were flying it, and we were confident.

It was one of the greatest games I've ever seen, let alone been involved with. Gooch gave an exhibition and Kerry were fantastic in the first half; Diarmuid Connolly and Dublin came back strong in the second.

I got on for the last 13 minutes. I picked up Eoghan O'Gara and was satisfied with my involvement.

People will remember the closing stages. A ball breaking around midfield. Michael Darragh Macauley diving in to win it. Kevin McManamon taking off with the ball.

Myself and Eoin Brosnan were in front of him and we thought he was going for a point, but it dipped under the bar. Goal. They came with that late surge and we couldn't hold them out.

At the final whistle I felt as though nothing had been gained. All the sacrifices, my push to recovery, my endurance of pain, my mental and physical torture, refusing advice from my nearest and dearest – all of that hardship just to experience a loss? The prospect of getting to the All-Ireland final was within my grasp with 13 minutes to go in the game, and then it was gone.

I could see the disappointment in Éamonn too. He had done so well in his first year but he bleeds the green and gold and a defeat like that would go deep.

For me it was a matter of convincing myself that the injury wasn't going to define me, that I still had unfinished business.

The following year I'd be 34, but I'd learned the benefits of that pre-season work. If I were to have any chance of playing in the championship in 2014 I had to do well in the league. If I were to have any chance of playing in the league I had to put that work in.

Two weeks after the Dublin game I was in the gym hitting it hard.

16

Mayo Twice in a Week

After a stop-start year I couldn't wait to get back in 2014. Every player is a creature of habit, basically, and I was no different. The off-season was now my pre-season, so I hit the gym.

I could also accept that the gym, fitness and keeping myself in shape were all becoming part of my identity. I really enjoyed going to the gym and loved the fitness work, quite apart from using it as a base for football.

For 2014, I was waiting for a call from Éamonn, and thankfully it came. We had a good chat. He mentioned that I'd been very unlucky with injuries in 2013, that as a team we'd come up against a great Dublin side at their peak in one of the greatest games ever.

While he was talking, my mind was ticking over. Tomás had retired, Eoin Brosnan had retired, and I was looking down the barrel of 34 years of age. There were plenty of young lads putting their hands up, and Éamonn believed in giving youth its chance, which was very fair.

Eventually the conversation came to 2014, and he asked me what my plans were. I was straight up: I wanted to come back and I wanted to start on the team. It wasn't a question of just wanting a jersey: I made it clear that I was willing to fight for a jersey. I had the mindset.

A player wants to play, full stop: no matter how much he can add to the positivity within the group, if he's being honest he wants to start every game.

Is that selfish? It is, but sport is selfish. It's all about you, the player – until you get to the game, and then it's about the team and the group.

On Éamonn's side he thought – or at least I hoped he did – that I was a positive influence around the camp, even when I'd been injured, but he'd have known well that every player wants to start.

Was I nervous that the conversation might take a different tack, along the lines of 'Thanks, but we're going in a different direction with different players'?

Of course, and that message would have been accepted, coming from someone like Éamonn.

Every time a manager comes in he brings new ideas; you never see a managerial appointment announced or discussed without the words 'freshening up' being used, and that usually means P45s for a number of players.

It's a delicate situation. I wanted to stay but at the same time I wasn't the kind of person who would argue with management.

Having said all that, it was good hearing him say that he thought I had more to offer and that it would be great if I stayed on. That was music to my ears after the year I'd had, the knocks and setbacks: it was a great boost to get and I was willing and able for the challenge.

Now, he probably thought I was stone mad as well, trying to get back after breaking an elbow, but at least that meant that when I told him I'd leave no stone unturned, he knew I meant it. I was ready to apply myself 100 per cent.

Éamonn also said management would be looking at youth and new players for 2014. I knew the group was getting a good influx of youth – Paul Murphy, Mikey Geaney, Stephen O'Brien, Alan Fitzgerald, and Daithí Casey and Johnny Buckley from Crokes – there was a bit of steel about them, and when they came in, the grit they brought definitely added to the mix and made players work that bit harder.

They'd challenge you in training, which is exactly what you want. If you gave one of them a clip, they wouldn't back off, which is the kind of preparation every player needs in the game.

And if those lads came through in the league and were good enough, they'd get jerseys. That was fair enough because it showed me – and everyone else – where we stood. Those were the criteria and they'd be applied across the board.

To reach that standard and claim a jersey I had to really put it in when it came to the gym and I savoured every minute of it.

Here's the difference: you can go to the gym and tell yourself you're doing the work, but at that level it has to be more focused. You must be conscious that you're in the gym getting ready to play for Kerry. And when I got off the call I made that commitment to myself – that I'd get myself good and ready for 2014.

Brendan Kealy and I did a lot of that work together in the winter of 2013. Brendan was the Kerry goalkeeper at the time and one of my closest friends on the team. We saw a lot of the small pitch in Killarney at that time – and Denise would fall in with us a few nights to train as well. She and I would do sprints with a common goal of fitness and it's fair to say we were slightly competitive at times.

I had the keys to the gym in Fitzgerald stadium so we'd go in, hit the gym, then come out and do our 400s, our 200s and so on; it was easier to start that training in November rather than face it for the first time in January.

That early training stood to me so much. It meant that, going into the league, I was in good shape, as opposed to being on the back foot when the hard training began in January, trying to hang onto the pack during the punishing runs.

I'd been driven before, but from 2012 I thought much more about my approach to playing. My drive now was different – I broke down my strengths and weaknesses far more, even though I kept that analysis to myself: I wasn't broadcasting my views to all, I just focused on getting myself absolutely right.

My basic motivation was to have no regrets about 2014. If I got beaten or didn't have a good game because an opponent got the better of me, that was perfectly fair, but it wouldn't happen for want of preparation.

Despite that, there was a familiar feel to the league in 2014. It was like being in a time machine and going back to my start with Kerry, looking at the jersey numbers to figure out where I'd fit in best.

Guys like Paul Murphy were putting their hands up immediately and it was clear that there was going to be real competition for places.

The only setback was the injury to Gooch with his club, but as a group it made us stronger and more driven and we were not going to leave any stone unturned in our pursuit to get to an All-Ireland final – so that Gooch could have the chance to be back and play in it.

We went on a training camp that year to Portugal and it was really beneficial and enjoyable. There was a meeting at the end of that camp and I can remember saying to Cian O'Neill, who was the physical trainer, that I thought we could get fitter.

He gave me a look as if to say, 'Are you questioning me?' – which I wasn't by any means, but I knew the personalities and the characters we had in the group and felt we could get to a level we hadn't reached before.

The science was part of that. I can remember being on the bus with Cian going back to the airport to come home to Ireland, and he was running through my results from the physical testing we had done.

He was saying, 'This is your score ... this is the average ... this is the highest score ...'

I should have been taking my age into account when he was showing me those figures, but I could only see the top figures, the top performers, and I was saying to myself, *That's where I need to be.*

I'd had a very good pre-season in terms of training and fitness and was in good shape, but guys like Donnchadh Walsh and Paul Geaney were hitting massive scores on those tests.

From what he learned in 2013, I felt that in 2014 Éamonn was determined to make the team tougher mentally. We started back after Portugal, the first night in April, with 400-metre runs in Killarney, and on the eighth or ninth run I began to realise why I was comparing myself to the youngest/fastest on the team.

I was wondering if Cian O'Neill was giving me a

message about questioning whether the team could get fitter, and being as stubborn as I was, there was no way I was going to back down from a challenge like that.

Dr Mike Finnerty caught sight of me and said, 'Hey, you look pale,' and he told me to drop out for a run. But I couldn't do that – I held on for the last one, the twelfth.

It was obvious that the young players were driving it on. Players like Peter Crowley and Stephen O'Brien were putting in an extreme effort, and everyone else was matching that – there was nobody waiting for anyone else.

Those three or four weeks were unreal. Out of my entire career, I'd often pick out that period for the sheer effort that was being made. There were spectators who'd wander into Crokes' pitch, where we were training, and they'd see these guys giving absolutely everything to get a jersey.

When I say 'everything', I mean it. We had spoken as a group of getting to a place we hadn't been before collectively. That wasn't to discard the element of sports science, but we wanted to go through that hardship to get ourselves right and also to gel as a group.

And we did gel as a result of it.

For instance, we went up to the Galtee mountains for a day with the army rangers. There was an itinerary given out and one of the items every player had to bring was Heinz baked beans.

I rang Marc Ó Sé and said, 'We're going to be landed into the middle of some bog somewhere and we'll be starved with the hunger, so bring as many tins of beans as you can carry. And tell everyone else in the group to do the same.'

I was working that night so I drove up, and when I got out of the car a ranger told me to get in line straight away. I saw Mikey Sheehy, who was a selector, roaring laughing off to one side, but I fell in, backpack on the shoulders, and we were sent off on a 5-kilometre run to a farmhouse up the mountain.

The tins were like blocks bouncing around in the backpack as we set off, and it was the longest 5K we ever ran.

It was both funny and brutal at the same time. There were group challenges, but what made it was that everyone took those challenges seriously. Those kinds of team exercises work if the entire group buys into them and applies themselves to them, and that group certainly did.

I saw a completely different side to players like Johnny Buckley and Mikey Geaney, guys who'd eat you without salt on the field but who showed how they could work together in a different environment. We were doing runs around the field in a group, say, with everyone hanging onto a small rope – nobody waiting for anyone else – to show that everyone was pulling together.

We finished off the day with a treasure hunt: in our case the 'treasure' was a 10-kilogramme medicine ball. The reward for finding it was lugging it up to the top of another one of the Galtee mountains, which were losing their appeal fairly fast at that stage.

Some of the players – I'm not saying they were lightweights – were half-fried from the experience by then but they thought the bus would be at the top of the last mountain we had to run up, so they carried on.

When we got there we were exhausted. On the top of that last mountain Éamonn handed out Kerry jerseys to us. The whole exercise was a brilliant recreation of what it's like at the end of a game, when you're out on your feet but you know you've got to keep going and get over the line somehow. The most important thing I took from it was that no matter what your mountain is, no matter how physically or mentally tired you are, if you're part of a group that sees no boundaries, the world is your oyster.

Éamonn said a few words, we took a few pictures – and then we had to run all the way back down, despite the rumours of a bus being at the summit to rescue us.

It was a day to get through but it was a great lesson. It showed everyone the benefits of just hanging in there, of surviving to the very end. And it showed us that the group is stronger than any individual.

(The individuals take a bit longer to recover than the

group, though. I had to drive back afterwards to go to work – rather than being able to take time out to recover at home – and when I got into the patrol car my legs started to cramp up.) We were asked, of course, where we'd gone for the day, and soon enough we were hearing stories about us pushing bales of hay around the fields of Tipperary when we'd have been better off playing county league. Rumours again.

That block of training galvanised the group. The camp in Portugal, the three or four weeks of intense workouts, the day in the Galtee mountains ... to this day if I meet any of the guys who soldiered through that period, it's like a mark of respect between us all that we did that work and came out the other side. It helped to open the year out for us.

We were up against Clare, who were a coming force under Colm Collins, a very good manager. For me it was all about starting the game and performing to my maximum ability. Looking around the dressing room I felt there were many in the group capable of winning an All-Ireland, and the weekend before Clare we had an internal game, A versus B.

I was doing very well at full-back with the A team but after 50, 55 minutes I saw a few of the other older players going off, their work done, while I stayed on. Pauly O'Donoghue came on and kicked 1–1 or 1–2 in 10 or 15 minutes off me.

Not good. As I say, there's a school of thought that you might be better off on the B team because you've less to lose, but the A team had done well and I'd had a good 45 to 50 minutes anyway.

We trained the following Tuesday night, and on those nights – the week of a game – members of the management had a habit of sitting up on the wall near the tunnel leading out onto the field.

That had an effect on the guys in the dressing room. Instead of the normal routine of being out on the field thirty minutes or an hour before training, players would be in no rush out in case Éamonn called them over for a chat. Which was never a good sign.

On this particular night, having delayed as long as we could, everyone jogged out.

'Aidan.'

Éamonn was calling me over.

'Look,' he said, 'we're not going to start you on Sunday.'

He explained management's thinking behind it, but I wasn't really listening. It's about yourself in a moment like that, as it's so difficult not to be disappointed.

You can't go around looking and feeling negative at training because you'd risk harming the team. I was devastated at the time but a good training session before a championship game was too important to be spoiled by my disappointment.

As I left that evening Éamonn said to pick up the phone

if I wanted to chat, and the following day I decided to ring him.

We had a chat and I made the point that I could have come out of the A v. B game after 50 minutes if I wasn't so stubborn, but instead I'd stayed on, being overly ambitious, and that action had made the call to drop me an easy one.

He didn't agree, and we went back and forth on it, but he had the last word, which was accepted: 'We went with a decision, but be ready for Sunday because you will be needed on the pitch.'

When you believe in management and have so much respect for them, you take that on board. Good thing I did, because after 23 minutes I was on against Clare, and I held onto my place for the Munster final against Cork.

There were lessons there for me. If I'd argued and confronted management's decision after hearing I was on the bench, and then carried a bad attitude around for the week … if I'd been put on after 23 minutes in those circumstances I would probably have been very poor and confirmed the management's decision to drop me in the first place.

James O'Donoghue and Declan O'Sullivan were outstanding in the Munster final against Cork. I was playing wing-back. We played Galway in the All-Ireland quarter-final. I was stationed at wing-back and that's where I was for the Mayo games, which are the games a lot of people still remember when they think of that particular season.

We were wary of Mayo. They'd probably have thought they were unlucky in 2013 and that they had a score to settle; we'd been in the same situation ourselves and we knew the only way to eliminate the hurt of losing a final was to get back and win one.

Mayo were very strong down the spine of the team, and they also had lads who were well suited to particular match-ups, like Keith Higgins, who'd pick up James O'Donoghue.

In the game itself we ended up straying from the game plan: we sat back too much and let Mayo come on to us. Lee Keegan was sent off for them, and even though we had a free man, we dropped back too much.

We were four up at half-time but they came into it and drove at us; they had the momentum and they were on top. I ended up coming off with 10 or 15 minutes to go but it seemed to be going away from us. We were losing by five points with time running out.

As it happens, a few weeks before then I'd texted Kieran Donaghy, who hadn't been getting much game time. I'd told him I'd been in that position more than once, on the outside looking in, and I was telling him to hang in there, that I knew he'd end up making a massive contribution to the cause. At the time he was probably thinking, *Would he ever leave me alone*, but I could remember as a young guy how much a message could mean, how encouraging it could be.

I'd have done the same for a player who might have felt he deserved my spot, because you have to think of the team and what's best for the team – and a player who feels isolated or forgotten if he's not starting isn't what's best for the team.

With a few minutes left in Croke Park I was looking out at the field thinking we needed a miracle, and Éamonn sent Kieran in. The move paid off – a long ball dropped into the square and the best man to catch it was there: Donaghy. The best man to come onto his pass was there as well – James O'Donoghue was on fire that year and he buried the goal. Kieran O'Leary, a man for the big day, levelled it up and we came close to a winner a couple of times in injury time, which people tend to forget. What they remember is the drama of James's goal, which was no surprise, and even as we headed out of Croke Park I was thinking it was the greatest escape of all time.

On the Tuesday I headed to Santry for an injection in my right ankle, which affected my training. I wanted to train on the Thursday but they told me to rest it and I'd be right for the replay on the Saturday.

There were plenty of other distractions going on anyway. The sideshow of going to Limerick for the replay, for instance.

I'd picked up Aidan O'Shea for part of the first day, and he's a fair test. Peter Crowley picked him up the second day, when Aidan moved to the 40, and did very well on him; Peter has plenty of steel to him.

Mayo had plenty of quality elsewhere too. Cillian O'Connor, Seamie O'Shea in midfield, Keith Higgins, Colm Boyle, Lee Keegan. Great players, but we were confident going up to Limerick that day.

Éamonn dropped Marc Ó Sé for that particular game and Marc showed his class all week at training. He was unreal – for a man who had been dropped for probably the first time in his life, he really set the tempo and drove training all that week.

For all the complaining about the venue – there was an American football game being played in Croke Park – it was like playing a match above in Castlebar: forget the crowd being a sixteenth man: they were up to about the eighteenth man.

During the pre-match warm-up we could see that there were empty spaces in the stands and the terraces, but when we came back out they'd been filled with Mayo supporters – I'd say it was four or five to one in their favour.

They showed it in the game. They banged in 2–2 inside a few first-half minutes but what stays with me is that we didn't flinch. No-one's head dropped. Shane Enright pulled down Cillian O'Connor for a penalty; O'Connor scored from that and he got another goal soon after.

But we got back. Donaghy was crucial. He got a goal and we were only three behind at half-time, but scores apart, it was an extraordinary game. I think it was the only time that I played a game at that level where positions really meant nothing.

Marc Ó Sé came on and early in the second half he went up the field and kicked a super point, and it was a real message. Anthony Maher and David Moran were out of this world that day – they did so much tough work for everyone else to shine – while Donnchadh Walsh, as usual, ran himself into the ground for the team, one of the most unselfish and inspiring players I've ever come across. But it was one of those games where everyone is absolutely committed to it.

It was a game that dragged everything out of you. At the very end, Mayo goalkeeper Rob Hennelly came down the field to take the free that might have won it for them, but Donaghy rose highest to catch it. Extra time.

We took the game to them but it was unbelievable: all over the field fellas were trying things they'd never try normally, myself included. At one stage Jason Doherty was going through and I just flung my body across him and got my hands on the ball somehow. Another day you wouldn't think of trying it but that was the level everybody was at, just trying everything they could and putting their bodies on the line.

Still, by about 83 minutes I could tell the body was

gone, I felt the hamstrings and quads beginning to cramp up. But a ball broke from a kick-out – I could see six pairs of Mayo socks in front of me, and I dived in to try and win it.

I won a free and we got upfield for a score, but I was gone. My legs were cramping up badly and Dr Mike Finnerty and Eddie Harnett carried me off – things were so chaotic, I'd say it was a case of 'Just get him off' – and Jonathan Lyne from Legion came on and was one of the heroes of the day, floating over two massive scores from distance when the game was in the melting pot.

Then you had the Mayo supporter coming onto the field – he was going for the Kerry players … it was one of the most entertaining games of all time for spectators.

One of my strongest memories is of Marc Ó Sé doing three or four Séamus Darby-type leaps in the air at the final whistle. Lads were on their knees, absolutely drained. Those two games tested everyone to the limit.

We had a bit of luck in the game as well, but as I always say, you need that. Aidan O'Shea and Cillian O'Connor ran into each other, then Rob Hennelly's free being fielded by Kieran. It was just a special game to be part of because it made us as a group.

We were on the bus afterwards looking at each other and thinking, *Did all of that really happen?*

We knew we'd been in a real battle and everyone had contributed. Everyone had fought on their backs for the team, from Jonathan Lyne coming on to hit two points, to James O'Donoghue, Donaghy and Paul Geaney's performances in the full-forward line, making things happen.

Everything began to combine and to pull the group even closer. The training in Crokes at the start of the year, the trip to the Galtee mountains, the two games with Mayo … it was all helping to drive the group to where we wanted to go.

Watching the other semi-final, a part of me wanted Dublin to come through so we could have another cut off them, but when Donegal won, that brought me back to 2012 and the conversation with my dad on the train, and the esteem in which he held Michael Murphy.

At the next Kerry training session I said to Éamonn that I wanted to mark Michael Murphy in the final. That was the mission, the vision and the challenge.

He said management would look at their match-ups, but what made training – and picking the team – very interesting in the run-up to the final was the fact that so many players had done so well against Mayo, but Donegal would present a particular challenge.

Every team has its approach, its pattern of play, and that was never truer than in Donegal's semi-final win over Dublin that year. Looking at it, I was thinking, *If I'm on Michael Murphy, is he going to be inside or will he move out the field?* Against Dublin they'd pulled their wing-forwards deep, playing a kind of blanket defence, but when they won the ball they all broke forward together. Defending against them you'd be thinking, *Who do I pick up when they all come forward?*

That was where Éamonn and his management team came into their own. They looked at that Dublin–Donegal game and saw that the Dublin wing-backs followed the Donegal wing-forwards back the field, leaving lots of space to hit Michael Murphy and Colm McFadden – who used runners coming off them to get the goals.

Going into the final, Éamonn and the management team were saying, 'Don't get sucked up the field after them, just keep your shape.' The instructions were straightforward: 'Aidan O'Mahony, you're picking up Michael Murphy; Paul Murphy, take Ryan McHugh; Marc Ó Sé, take Colm McFadden.'

The other big thing management focused on was getting Donaghy to put pressure on Paul Durcan's kick-outs, to force him to go long if necessary. We weren't trying to out-Donegal Donegal: we wanted to play our own system – but not to leave ourselves open. That was the key element.

If Michael Murphy went out over the sideline that day I was going to follow him: I was focused, I felt very fit, I was ready. But you can't help but be a little nervous as well – in this case because of his quality. He was the best footballer in the country that year, a complete player who could do it on his own and also improve his team-mates.

There was another element in it for me, of course. He was the last GAA player I'd spoken to my dad about in that final conversation I had with him, and here I was going in to mark him in the All-Ireland final.

My main focus was on trying to hold him, when he had the potential to cut loose and cause major problems for Kerry.

At a meeting before the game we discussed what we'd do in the game and I remember saying, 'I will mark Michael Murphy,' repeating that mantra three times.

At one level someone might say, 'That's putting pressure on yourself,' but it was a promise I had to make to the team. I wasn't going out to put him under pressure; I was going out to mark him out of game. The other promise – in honour and memory of my dad – had taken me nearly two years to fulfil, but the Sunday morning of the All-Ireland final I knew the time had come.

My attitude was simple: I had done everything that was required, my preparation had been 100 per cent, and I knew what I had to do in the game.

In the build-up I don't think many people had picked me out as a likely marker for Michael Murphy – at 34 there were probably doubts I'd have the power for him, the go-to guy for Donegal. I knew what the task involved, and that had to be a help.

Even though I'd been there before, All-Ireland final day is still an amazing experience. Shaking hands with the president, the other team filing past to shake hands, nobody blinking an eye.

Glance to the sideline: there's Jim McGuinness, looking completely composed. Éamonn a few yards away, equally calm.

That's a significant sight for any player before an All-Ireland final, because their composure filters through to you: they're calm, so I'll be calm.

Walking around the field was enjoyable for me, mostly because at 34 years of age I knew well there weren't too many days like this in my playing future.

I glanced back at Jim McGuinness and I thought again of the day above in Donegal when the snow was falling and he was roaring at his players to leave the ball in long on top of myself and Michael Murphy. I was thinking, *Yes, leave it in long on top of me today; I'm a different player now.*

From early on in the game I recognised what Michael was trying to do – come around on a loop, lose his man and get on the ball as his team-mates popped it out to him.

But my attitude had reverted back to what I'd brought into minor training with Kerry 16 years earlier: mark my man, keep the ball away from him and ignore everything else.

I tracked him all over the field. At one point he was chatting to Jim McGuinness over near the sideline and I was right there next to them. I couldn't tell you who else was there, because I was concentrating totally on Michael. I could hear the crowd laughing at the sight of the three of us, but that didn't have any impact on me.

Elsewhere the lads followed orders. Peter Crowley and Killian Young stayed at home in the half-back line and let their men drop away back the field if they wanted. Between the two 45s there was a war zone where both sides met their men, and our lads did well.

What many people will probably recall was the very end of the game, when our goalkeeper Brian Kelly got fingertips to the ball and pushed it onto the post. Shane Enright the north Kerry man was in the right place for the rebound and came out like a gladiator. We got that bit of luck, but I've said it before: every team needs that bit of luck to get over the line.

We got it that day. There were plenty of days when we didn't.

Gooch got injured early in 2014, when he damaged his knee in a club game. He got back and was togging out those last few weeks of the season with us. Declan O'Sullivan the same: he'd overcome injuries to remain part of the team, and when he spoke up in the dressing room you could hear the respect in the silence that met his words. Everything he said made sense.

Declan came on and helped steady the ship. Shane Enright came on to pick up Paddy McBrearty and quietened him late on. Bryan Sheehan came on and nailed a massive free.

When the final whistle went the emotion of the moment caught me. I hadn't been broadcasting the fact that I'd been working on an All-Ireland in memory of my dad.

The whole group was emotional, not surprisingly. That's the same for every team, but because those outside the group don't know what the players go through, it can be hard to convey, that sense of getting over the line together and what that means.

I got to walk up the steps of the Hogan stand and lift the Sam Maguire.

When I did I looked up at the sky and said, 'This one is for you, Dad.'

For myself, on the pitch after the game with Gooch, the cup between us … you have to remember the battles we had over the years, with Rathmore and Crokes, but the admiration is huge for him, and genuine, a guy who I would class as one of the greatest I have ever played with.

Walking down the Cusack stand side of the field, then, a young boy standing behind the wall caught my eye – he had a purple Kerry top on – and something made me stop. I took off my football boots, walked over and handed them to him. I shook hands, said hello and then carried on around the field.

We handed the cup onto Killian Young, strolled on and sat down with Donaghy for a chat on the field, watching the golden tinsel come down.

In the dressing room we came together, and Éamonn said a few words. It's an incredible moment. Every player has his own motivation for winning, and there's something special when you realise that every single person in the room has given absolutely everything for the cause.

And yet it all comes down to a kick of the ball in the last play of the game. That's how tight it is.

I was the last out of the dressing room that day. Before I left, the cup was next to me and I reminded myself to take this moment in.

In the early years I'd be in and out of the dressing room in a flash, and the occasion wouldn't have made any impression on me.

This was different. The change in a couple of years was huge, but the lesson for me was about perseverance. On a few occasions in the previous months I could have called it a day, but I kept going. I had that extra motivation, the challenge to myself, to keep me going.

Heading out to the hospital in Crumlin the morning after and the joy you see on people's faces when they see the cup. Having the chat with Marty Morrissey before we left the hotel and headed for the train. That day he made me presentable and fixed my bow tie and the media captured a classic picture of him doing so.

One of the real highlights was the journey back to Rathmore. Shane Ryan, a club-mate of mine, had won a minor All-Ireland with Kerry, so there were two cups coming back to the club.

The stops along the way and the sense we were coming closer and closer – it was the first time, really, I had to fight back tears, because when my family came to meet me on the train platform in Rathmore it was the first time my dad wasn't there with them. They were emotional. So was I.

We brought the cups up on stage – Paul Murphy had been named man of the match in the senior game, which was another feather in the cap for the club, Shane had the minor cup, there were thousands there … it was a huge occasion for all of us.

The train rolled on to Tralee – all my colleagues in the gardaí were there waiting for me (I had transferred to Tralee from Cork in May), the likes of Pat O'Sullivan, my boss, and so were 30,000 people on Denny Street. It was just an unforgettable occasion.

Before we went up on the stand, I got a phone call from someone from the media: was I aware that a video had gone viral in Ireland of me giving my boots away to a young boy in Croke Park? At that point I didn't know anything about it but vividly recalled the boy's face when I handed him the boots.

We had the GOAL game on the Wednesday night, but my ankle was in bits and I couldn't play. I did rock up in a Harry Styles-type shirt, though, which probably entertained more people than the game, particularly when I fell in for the picture.

That's a time when you can enjoy the little moments: myself, Gooch and Mikey Sheehy strolling along in Tralee and naming ourselves as a dangerous full-forward line. After the game walking down Tralee town and heading to Tom Quane's bar in Blenerville. It's a week you don't want to pass too quickly, but it doesn't last. Real life comes knocking fairly fast.

And sometimes that's not a bad thing.

I eventually learned that the boy I gave the boots to was named Diarmuid Willis. He has Angelman syndrome and sometimes he gets respite in Home from Home in Killarney, an after-school service for children with special needs.

People asked how I spotted him in the crowd after the final whistle; it was just pure luck that I went over to him. When I learned who he was, I got on to the county board for the Sam Maguire and brought it down to Home from Home for Diarmuid along with a bag of Kerry gear.

I got talking to his dad, Dick, and the staff, and they were saying that Home from Home was going through a rough enough time as an organisation with the recession.

They do great work and they needed some support, so I suggested they auction off the boots. The Kerry

Association in London had a function coming up and we thought that'd be the ideal place for the auction – Barry John Keane, one of the great characters in the Kerry panel, was going over and I asked him to bring the boots to Gerry Rochford and Eoin and Tara Cronin of the association, which he did.

The All-Stars banquet was on the same night but I didn't rate my chances of an award, so I didn't travel to Dublin. In any event I was getting into golf at that time and was due to play with David Hennebry at 6 a.m. the morning after the auction so I was in bed early that night when I got a phone call. Eoin Cronin was on the phone from the auction: 'Are you sitting down?'

'I'm in bed.'

'The boots got 24,000 pounds.'

I was silent. It didn't sink in at all. 'You mean 2,400 pounds?'

'No, I mean 24,000 pounds.'

I was shocked and overwhelmed. There were tears in my eyes. I was thanking him and he was telling me they'd auctioned the boots, and re-auctioned them, and more and more money had come in.

I rang Dick, Diarmuid's dad, and told him how much had been raised for Home from Home.

He was shocked. In fact he rang me back the following morning to confirm that the figure I'd told him was actually correct. He still couldn't believe it.

When the cheque landed at Home from Home the relief and joy in the place was unreal. It had all stemmed from something spontaneous. The real beauty of it is that the person who bought the boots actually went on to donate them to Home from Home, which was a fantastic touch.

Over the years I'd have often donated jerseys for charity. I'd be very aware of being in a privileged position and if anyone rang me for something like that I'd do my best to help out. But this was on a totally different level.

It was something beautiful that put the cap on the year. I'd wanted to get up the steps and collect the cup, but the boots and the auction were the icing on the cake.

To this day it pops into my head: what made me stop at that particular point, as I went around the pitch, and go over to Diarmuid? I've no doubt it was my dad above, pointing the way so I could help somebody out.

I've needed help from others along the way, and it was time for me to help someone in turn. But the way it worked out was magical.

We sadly lost Denise's mom in 2011, then my dad passed away the following year.

I learned that when you want to do something in memory of someone, there might be obstacles in your way. But I also learned about drive and the real desire within me to do something in my dad's memory – and that I didn't need to share that motivation, necessarily. I could keep it to myself and for myself.

There were setbacks in 2012 and 2013 but they didn't stop me, and in 2014 it all fell into place. What happened with the boots and raising money for Home from Home showed me that if you really want to help someone, there's always a way.

17

Moving Out of My Comfort Zone

Dancing with the Stars

We lost to Dublin in the 2016 All-Ireland semi-final, and around October that year I got a call from Joe O'Connor of Nisus Fitness in Tralee.

He's also a referee on *Ireland's Fittest Family*. He mentioned that he was speaking to one of his contacts in ShinAwiL, the television production company, and that rehearsals for a new dancing show were due to start after Christmas. They were inquiring about the possibility of getting a Kerry GAA player involved. I was asked if I would express an interest in this and, not knowing any details, I agreed to sharing my contact details with the production company. I didn't think too much about it as I was concentrating on enjoying a different type of fitness and everyday training after the All-Ireland loss.

A week or so after my conversation with Joe O'Connor, Adam McGarry Byrne gave me a call. He introduced himself and gave me an overview of the show, called *Dancing with the Stars*, and what was involved. After some further chat he asked me if I'd be interested in taking part, and I told him I would think about it.

There followed a few Zoom calls with members of the production team, and I was persuaded to say 'yes'. I knew my football career at inter-county level was coming to an end anyway so there would be no interference to my training, but there was something more than that which initiated my 'yes'.

I spoke to Denise about it and told her I could see all the reasons why I shouldn't do it, all the reasons why it wasn't for me – but she converted all of those into reasons why I *should* do it. She loves a challenge, and the more fearful, the better. As to what would actually be involved, Adam spelt it out for me: 'It'll be live on television on Sunday nights and it'll be the first of its kind in Ireland – but if you come in you'll have to be prepared to give it 21 hours a week training and rehearsing the routines.'

Manageable, I thought. I could arrange that with work. Chatting to Denise about it, we reckoned that 21 hours of rehearsing was equivalent to three days' work, which was a bit of a stretch if I had to go and base myself in Dublin: what if I could do two 10-hour days instead, which sounded more manageable? If so, I wouldn't have to go to Dublin until a day later.

Adam and Eugenia Cooney got back to me over another video call and this time we had a longer chat – not so much an interview as getting to know each other a bit better. At the time, I was preparing for a charity dancing event for Down Syndrome Kerry, and in my mind I was thinking, *This is going to be much the same thing: a bit of fun, exercise and a positive challenge.*

When I asked about the other contestants involved, Adam wasn't giving anything away, which made me a bit anxious. It was all very confidential and there were no details disclosed of numbers, partners, presenters or competitors. If I'd known there were people lined up that I knew personally it would have been a good incentive to mentally prepare myself.

But even taking all of that into consideration – that I might know no other contestant or the standard required for dancing at that level – I flipped things around. Instead of taking those as reasons to be reluctant, I reminded myself that the unknown is something that I had to become familiar with.

I had spent the past number of Christmases away with Denise and family and this year was no different – a 12-day trip had already been planned. Adam had mentioned that being away right before the show shouldn't be a big issue but that I'd have to learn a single dance and a group dance for the first week of January. I had a great holiday in the sunshine and didn't for a second think about what was ahead of me.

There was a 'meet and greet' with all the contestants ahead of the names being announced. Slowly, I found out who the others were. I was delighted to see Des Cahill from RTÉ among them, because I knew him through the football and expected a bit of banter about Kerry and Dublin and Gaelic football generally. I had great respect for Des, and I was less anxious knowing I would see one familiar face at least.

On the first day of filming we had to record our introductions. Before I even got to the studio I was much more anxious than walking out for an All-Ireland final. On the journey to Bray, I questioned my choice and wondered what I'd got myself into.

On top of the unique nerves there was a sense of having missed my chance to get ahead of the curve years before. When I was a kid in national school we had an Irish dancing teacher who came in to give us lessons, but after just one lesson she advised me to stick to the football. I was perfectly fine with that back then, but fast-forward 30 years and I'm thinking I should have given it a little more time. All my brothers and sisters had done Irish dancing and set dancing for years, which is very strong in our home place. They are all excellent traditional dancers. A few steps would definitely be useful now, I was thinking, and would give me some confidence at least.

I had never had any interest in dancing, yet here I was bearing down on a TV studio where I'd be showing off my best steps to hundreds of thousands of people watching live on television over the next three months. No pressure.

When I reached Ardmore Film Factory, I pulled up to the steel gates and was greeted by security. From the outside it didn't look too busy but when I went inside there were dozens of people milling around.

Putting up lights, working cameras, taking photographs, people on microphones and walkie-talkies: there must have been a couple of hundred people working on the programme and sets.

I could see a green backdrop at one end of the studio – publicity photographs being taken by Jenny McCarthy – but what caught my eye was a long catwalk in one corner of the factory sparkling with mini glitter-balls.

In all honesty, for a second or two I thought about tiptoeing back out the door and driving back to Kerry. But instead I just rolled with it and settled into the environment. I had to focus on what was ahead.

Everyone was extremely welcoming; the ShinAwiL staff were quick to introduce themselves – and the other contestants. I knew Des Cahill, and I'd seen Des Bishop in a few live gigs, but most of the others were new acquaintances to me, though we became great friends over the course of the show.

I was brought off by the stylists to be given my costume. I'd already been measured for it, and they took those measurements very seriously: the costume looked like I'd been poured into it, the fit was so tight.

When I saw the green velvet blazer and green bling dicky bow I knew I'd be hearing about my fashion choices for a while. At that point only my family and Denise knew I was involved in the show, but I anticipated plenty of commentary from lads on football fields around Kerry after the first broadcast.

Then I headed in to Liffey Trust Studios to meet Valeria Milova, who would be my dance partner. It's a funny setup – almost unnatural – because the cameras are there to record your first impressions of each other for the show, so the whole thing is captured for posterity. We chatted and got to know a little about each other. Then Valeria said, 'Okay, let's get started and try a few basic moves.'

At that stage I hadn't had the chance to explain to her that she'd been landed with an inter-county footballer who was like a statue when he wasn't doing what he'd been doing for 20 years. Gaelic football didn't serve me as well on the dance floor as you might think. A casual viewer might conclude that footwork and balance would be common to sport and dancing, but at that point the emphasis in Gaelic football was on conditioning above almost everything else.

As a result, the transition to an art-like form of dancing – movement, rhythm, relationship with lyrics, reacting to beat, muscle coordination, motion intelligence – was somewhat difficult. Dancing wasn't just totally unfamiliar to me: it was the exact opposite of the physical movement I'd been doing for years.

Anyway, after my first few moves, Valeria said, 'Oh no.'

I said, 'Oh no, that bad?'

'No,' she said, 'oh no, very bad.'

Well, I thought, things can only get better.

Back out to the studio in Ardmore for the publicity shots. Plenty of instruction from the photographer – 'Try this pose', 'Move this way' – and even though I was trying to look natural, it was so unnatural and outside of my comfort zone, I had to bring all the dramatics, something I wasn't that familiar with.

By now I was beginning to feel a little uncomfortable: on the football field or in the gym I always felt natural, and this was anything but.

Still, after the photo shoot we all got together properly, and I met Teresa Mannion, Thalia Heffernan and Katherine Lynch. And also Dr Eva, who gave me a signed copy of her best-selling diet/cook-book, which would come in handy in the weeks ahead. All participants were pretty nervous but at least some of them had a background in media, performing arts, presenting or acting of some type. They had some expectation of what was to come. Such as the catwalk requirements. There was a producer there from the UK and he told us to head up onto the catwalk and show off our best moves as we walked out, because they were filming it as an advertisement for RTÉ. Myself and Des had a good laugh. The whole group had to go up on the catwalk together and throw some shapes to the song 'Move Your Body' by Sia. Dance like there's no-one watching was far from the case. At this time I was so regretful I hadn't taken Denise up on all her invitations to dance salsa around the kitchen at home!

The glitter came down, and we were able to take a break. I had the charity dancing gig in Killarney that evening, and I told the lads in ShinAwiL that I had to head off early. But just when I thought I was free I was told they needed to do individual out-takes.

'Where's the Kerry GAA guy? He has to go first if he's leaving early.'

My worst nightmare: being sent up to dance before anybody else, showcasing just how far I had to go. I fought a rearguard action, asking the producer if it was fair to show me because we were all, you know, trying to learn from scratch exactly how to dance.

'Get up there and dance,' was his response.

The sweat was running down my back as I went to

the back of the catwalk because I had no idea what was expected, or what I could do. From the back of the stage to the camera at the front it was about 20 feet, and I got a brainwave.

I took a run out at the camera, jumped in the air and kicked my feet as high as I possibly could. The camera caught me in mid-air. All my plyometric training had paid off! I was pretty chuffed with myself as the nervous adrenaline almost sent me through the studio roof.

The producer just looked up at me and then to the other contestants. 'Now that's a good powerful standard to start off with – if everyone can do as well as that it'll be outstanding.'

Going first wasn't all that bad after all.

Before I could get away from the studio that day, an RTÉ interviewer, James Patrice, one of the most dramatic characters in showbiz and who really knows how to have a laugh during an interview, approached me. 'Well, Aidan O'Mahony, what are you thinking?'

'I'm thinking, "What can I possibly do to plan for this commitment? I cannot plan the unplannable."'

I laughed a lot, he laughed a lot, and Des then joined our interview and we had a bit of slagging over Kerry v. Dublin on the dancefloor, as expected.

At that time of course the competitor came out in me. No different to when I had come into the Kerry minor team years earlier, I was looking at the competition, but there wasn't much comfort in doing that in this context.

I was out of my depth, frankly, compared to some of the others who had a background in the performing arts. But there was another part of me that contextualised the potential experience and compared *Dancing with the Stars* to times with Kerry when I might have pushed myself further and out of my comfort zone. What would have happened if I hadn't done that?

Now I had the chance to do something that was a long way beyond my comfort zone. Why not go for it?

There were other considerations. We were building our house back in Killarney, and Denise was expecting. Here I was above in Dublin, doing something I'd never considered doing.

I remember the show was described as featuring 11 celebrities. I'm not a celebrity by name, and that tag didn't sit well with me. I remember Des saying at the time – when the list of participants, or celebrities, was released – that he and I would probably get a bashing and be described as Z-listers.

He was right about the bashing, but in all honesty that didn't bother us. I knew I'd be on holidays when the list was released anyway, away from the limelight.

But still, when I got myself onto the M50 that day and headed back to Kerry, I couldn't help but think of the line, '11 celebrities and their pro dancers'.

When I got home and Denise asked what it was like, I said it was one hundred times a bigger production than I'd expected: the glitter, the lights, the bling, the size of the set, the feedback on your dancing, the cameras with you all the time and the overall professionalism of the team.

That's something viewers don't pick up on when it comes to a show like that: you have people filming you all the time. And I mean all the time, for perhaps one to four minutes of footage.

At least I didn't have them screening my footsteps at the charity event in Killarney the evening I came home. I remember the MC asking me that night if they'd see me in a Kerry jersey again in 2017 – or maybe I'd be doing something else? After the day I'd just put down, it was definitely something else, but I couldn't yet disclose.

'You never know,' I said, playing it straight.

Ironically, he said, 'Sure you might take up the dancing after tonight's performance.' There was a big laugh from the packed crowd in the INEC.

'You'd never know,' I replied. I had a big grin on my face walking off the stage. If they only knew that what he had asked me as a joke was about to become a reality in a few weeks on live television.

At this stage, we had three weeks to our first dance in early January, but stripping it back to basics, my first thought was how it was going to work in terms of me getting to Dublin for rehearsals. So I worked Monday through to Wednesday, then I'd head up to Dublin on Thursday around lunchtime and rehearse that day and Friday. Looking back I was probably horizontally relaxed about the whole thing in comparison to the other contestants and their level of commitment and their invested time.

Initial rehearsals were for a salsa. One bit of luck was that Valeria's husband Vitali was another one of the pro dancers – he was partnered with Aoibhín Garrihy – so he and Valeria would do the routines for myself and Aoibhín, and then we'd go off to different rooms to rehearse separately on our own dances.

The first thing I said to Valeria was, 'Half of the stuff the two of you were doing – that just isn't going to happen.'

But she'd break it down. Start off with the steps – because the salsa is all about the steps – and put the hours in on that. When I say hours, I mean hours that were squeezed in together.

It was like a great coaching session, one you could apply to life. More than once early on in the rehearsals I was thinking, *I don't know if I'll get the hang of this – maybe I should pack it in.*

But Valeria would just say, 'Go again. Do it again. And again. And again.'

I don't think she ever once said she was unsure or doubtful I'd get it – she was hugely positive from the start. We'd do the steps and then we'd move on to a flip or a lift. That had me worried on a whole other level, not because I couldn't lift – I could do lifts all day everyday – but because I was thinking she'd break her neck if I dropped her.

But it was amazing the way it started to come together over a few days – you get the hang of the steps and then you get used to the music and feel the beat and relate that to the muscle.

The camera guys were there for a lot of it; they were filming all the rehearsals and interviewing everybody for the VT takeouts for the live show – you had to give a 30-second description of what you were planning to do so that it could be shown beforehand every Sunday night before you took to the dance floor. They might ask me about bringing in that competitive element, but while I'd point out that my competitiveness was in football, not dancing, you have to be true to yourself as well, to be accountable about who you are. And the competitiveness was kicking in.

Because I was over-nighting for rehearsals, the production company had accommodated me in an apartment in Spencer Dock. I remember my first night and there was a young lad there sharing with me. That was Dayl Cronin. We introduced ourselves, and I went off to put my bag away. As soon as I was in my room, of course, I was googling his name (and as he said to me later, he was doing the same in his own room). Perhaps the Z-listing was not a myth! We joked about that as the weeks went on.

I found out he was in a boy band, so I felt he'd have a good head start when it came to the dancing.

He's a great fella, very bubbly and friendly, and we got on really well despite the age gap. We chatted away that first evening about our backgrounds, and I was in awe when he was telling me about being in the band and all his live performances – and, of course, thinking I wouldn't hold a candle to someone with that kind of expertise in the field.

It was enjoyable too to be sharing with someone who had that kind of energy after a week at work. We developed a great friendship over the weeks of hanging out in the apartment and heading in for rehearsals, watching each other's dances.

And as things moved on, rather than thinking it wasn't for me, I was becoming more confident and getting the sense that Valeria felt there was some potential in my dancing – that I was a work in progress rather than a dead loss. My fitness was key in the rehearsals and I always felt there was more in the tank for the 'again, again and again'.

I had less than three weeks to get to grips with the dance, but there were other considerations as well, and the GAA wasn't long inserting itself into those considerations.

For instance, we had to get measured for costumes, and the place where we did so was a couple of doors up from The Boar's Head on Capel Street, one of the great GAA pubs in Dublin owned by the great Hugh Hourican.

Myself and Dayl would get the Luas down for the fitting and then pop in for a coffee with Hugh Hourican, who has become a friend for life. So that GAA life was still there too and the long chats that went with it; I might have been immersed in the world of dance but the world of Gaelic games wasn't too far away either, as was always the case.

Sometimes the trip to The Boar's Head was needed more than others. I remember being fitted for the first night's dancing, and the top they handed me was see-through.

That was bad enough, but the costume people weren't finished yet.

'Yeah, we'll have to cut back the sleeves ... we can make that tighter too ...'

I was thinking, *What on earth is my mom going to make of this get-up on my first night?* But nevertheless, when I got into my car to head back to Kerry, I felt I was enjoying it, and I was excited for the first show.

It was something new, and it was a beautiful time for myself and Denise anyway, expecting our first child and looking forward to our last holiday as two at Christmas. The day we headed to the airport for that trip was the day I revealed on social media that I would be on the show.

I remember saying to Denise on that holiday that people were going to get a bit of a surprise when they saw the show. The scale of the production was massive, and I'd seen the work that ShinAwiL and especially its CEO Larry Bass were putting into it.

I'd heard so many times about the void in players' lives after retiring from inter-county action that I was half-expecting to feel at a loose end, but there wasn't time to experience a void as I grappled with the challenge of the salsa.

I'd gone from having zero interest in or knowledge of dancing to really enjoying it, to the extent that I was comfortable with the other contestants coming in to watch our rehearsals. That was daunting, having other dancers come in. But they were hugely positive and encouraging – they'd watch and say, 'That's excellent,' and you'd do the same for them. People don't see that, but it's a huge boost, because a few days later you would be on your own in front of over 200 people in a live audience and three judges, all within touching distance.

As the first Sunday of the show itself approached, another reality began to sink in – the prospect of the opening sequence. This was a group dance involving all the contestants, and although I knew it would be great fun, there was a serious side to it also.

We all knew we'd be judged on our first dance by everyone, and I wanted people to come away thinking that, although I came in from a GAA background, I was making a decent fist of this dancing business as well.

We rehearsed on the Saturday in Ardmore Film Factory, the day before the live show, and getting there at six in the morning certainly made it real. All the camera people were there ready to go, the studio was set up, the judges' box was glistening but empty. My heart definitely skipped a beat at that stage.

You have a slot on the floor to perform your routine a few times; this time it's the actual dance floor and not the studio. You make mistakes, you're missing steps that you've been making without a problem for the last three weeks, you've half an eye out for the cameras and where they are … the difference was obvious straight away between someone like me and those who'd been performers or working in the media. Even something as straightforward – or apparently straightforward – as picking out where the cameras were came naturally to them, as did the faces you need to make while dancing. It was amazing to see that level of experience in front of the camera.

When you're dancing in a particular way you need to portray a character, to tell a story, but Valeria gave me a good tip when we started. Instead of trying to dance and portray a character at the same time, she told me to just go out and enjoy the dance, and that approach worked particularly well with the salsa. I never tried to be an actor that I wasn't!

That first Saturday was intense. We had to rehearse our individual dances but we also had to prepare the group dance, and that wasn't always good for the ego. I was thinking I had a good handle on our dance, but when I saw the standard, it really made me aware of what I had to invest to compete with them. They were outstanding.

My goals were pretty modest that first Sunday: to remember my steps and just be me in front of the entire country. I was aware of the hype that was building across the media – ShinAwiL and RTÉ were promoting the show heavily – but I was pretty confident I'd get through it without too many errors at least.

Then a tap on the shoulder: 'Time for the spray tan.'

The what?

If I was expecting ridicule for dancing in a see-through top, spray tan was going to raise the ridicule to a whole new level, but there was no way out of it.

Everyone was getting it done. I had returned from the sun for the first show so I felt I didn't really need the spray tan that first week. But by the end of the run, getting the spray tan was the most natural thing in the world.

Myself and Dayl were laughing as we came away in the car, but with every kilometre we travelled back to Spencer Dock our skin seemed to be getting darker and darker. By the time we were in the apartment, though, we were too tired to care but our minds were still racing. These steps. Those steps. That lift and this lift. We were going through the routines and also wondering about the following day, the live performance. The training period was over and the apprenticeship had been served: now it was time to show what we'd learned.

There was pressure, definitely. For me, going into learn a skill that was completely alien was obviously a challenge, and I knew I had to perform once I'd committed to it. Denise and my family were coming up for the weekend and would take in the show.

The adrenaline that Sunday morning was on a par with waking up for an All-Ireland final. Dayl and myself hardly slept; we jumped into my car and headed for Ardmore, Ed Sheeran blaring 'Castle on the Hill'. There was complimentary transport organised for all the contestants but I preferred to be in the comfort of my own car, which was provided by my good friend Donagh Hickey as I was his brand ambassador for Renault.

There was a dress rehearsal, where the producers ran through everything that would be happening in the show. I was happy with how our own rehearsal went but when I saw some of the other couples dancing I just said, 'Wow.'

It's a long day, show day. The crew are in studio from 6.30 a.m. until the show starts that evening.

You have to pass the time somehow – I always had a laugh getting the hair and make-up done in the afternoon, getting pictures of each other and just chatting to everyone on set. I remember scrolling the phone to see when the national leagues were starting off: anything for a distraction.

But playing football was good preparation in one sense. The day of a big game, an All-Ireland final, can be a long one too. You've got all the training done and you just have to wait until the game itself. But you also have to save that energy for the throw-in, something I was used to doing.

We kept going through the steps as the time approached, and at stages the nerves would kick in and fade away again. My mantra would always have been that nerves were good, they helped you focus, but these nerves were different and weren't as helpful as I'd hoped.

The audience started to stream in then around five o'clock. The bustling crowds made the whole thing real: families and friends coming in to take their seats to watch you. My own family arrived and it was so reassuring to see them. I was not going to disappoint them, as some of them had made a four-hour trip from Kerry, a journey they would do again after the show. I was ready.

Then the crew wished us well, the costume team – two amazing ladies – made the final touches to the outfits, all contestants hugged each other and we wished each other the best of luck.

The group dance was first, which eased everyone into it. The main objective was to get your routine right when the camera focused on you. It started with the camera on Des Bishop, with Des Cahill, Hughie Maughan, Dayl and myself in a casino, *mar dhea*, and then it kicked off, and it flew past. The energy and excitement was unreal, a fantastic buzz.

After that it was a run back to change costume in time for the individual dances, and I approached it as though it were a man-marking job: I'd worked with the team but now it was up to me to deliver.

One thing that has stayed with me is the sheer tightness of the costume: it was as though I'd jumped off a cliff and landed right in the pants – they were clung to me. I was happy I'd done all that gym work in the previous months.

I could only imagine the comments my poor mom would hear in the local shop, but I snapped out of that when one of the crew said, 'Right, Aidan, you're coming on.'

There was a platform behind the main stage where I stood with Valeria and I could see the VT with my introductory clip, filmed weeks before, and then it was out onto the stage.

As part of my routine I had a football in my hand and I took a few solos with it and walked down the steps – Valeria was to come out and try to take the ball off me and then we'd be into the salsa routine.

One last bit of advice she gave me stuck in my head: 'If something goes wrong with the routine or one of the steps, just keep going, you never stop.'

The adrenaline was pumping, Pitbull's 'Fireball' was getting louder in the background, the crowd were electric and I actually enjoyed the routine. I love that song as it reminds me of part of my honeymoon on a stop-off in Miami, when we went to see Pitbull and P. Diddy on new year's eve. That was a salsa party to remember, according to my wife.

We started off well, the moves were smooth, and then we got to her back flip. There was potential for this to be a disaster but we got through it. The minutes flew and the whole routine went off well. We walked over to Amanda Byram, a co-host of the show. The sense of accomplishment was terrific because it was our very first dance. We looked over at the judges and the comments were positive: a bit of work to be done on the hips, relax a little more, but overall a dance well done for the first night.

I remember Julian Benson saying, 'I see you as a dark horse – you'll have that competitive edge from the sport and I think there's a bit about you with this competition.'

The comment about the hips resonated with me – I'd spent years trying to open up my hips playing football, after all – but then we were running off the floor and up to Nicky Byrne. He's such a successful guy in the industry who is so humble, and just lovely, positive company to be around.

He asked me to compare the dance stage with Croke Park and I pointed out that in Croke Park if you made a mistake in the first minute you had the rest of the game to redeem yourself, but if you made a mistake dancing there was only a minute and a half to make up for it. During the entire show I never rehearsed what I was going to say after my dances: I just went with the flow with my word choice!

Nicky was hopping off me about Dublin and Kerry and to be honest the banter was so refreshing and the feeling of relief so great, having completed the dance.

We did various media interviews afterwards, and my tan came up early on in a question. I had a line about being on holidays for two weeks, which was true.

Reality kicked in after all of that as I went back to Kerry for work the following day. On the drive down I was struck by how I had fallen into this, how I knew on one level it wasn't for me but on the other it was worth a shot for the experience. But as the road rolled on, another thought found its way in: *What will people actually think of me at home doing something beyond my comfort zone?*

I pulled into the Obama Plaza for a coffee and had a look at social media. The feedback on my performance was generally positive, which was great. I jumped back in the car and spent the rest of the trip wondering how far I could go in the competition.

Back in Kerry, I didn't have long to wait for a reaction. When I went into the public office in Tralee garda station the following morning there was a big picture of me in my dance costume up on the wall. And the ribbing wasn't long coming from my colleagues: 'Oh, the dancer is in. Did you design your own costume?'

I sank to my knees laughing at the blown-up image of me. I had to give the lads what they wanted, so I told them that yes, I had picked it out myself, see-through and barely there. I loved the banter.

That was a big help to me, that routine and normality of getting back to work every Monday morning. People were good to me too, saying how well I'd done the previous weekend.

Myself, Dayl and Des Cahill had a great bond, while Aoibhín was dancing with Valeria's husband Vitali, so we were together a lot in the studio and we formed a great friendship throughout the show. It was an experience that you couldn't replicate – we were all trying to improve our skills, and while we were in competition with each other, there was great support for each other as well.

For me it didn't get competitive until week seven or eight: the first couple of weeks we had a quickstep, which was the first time I caught the brunt of it from Brian Redmond as a judge. I found the quickstep tough and he was saying it was a dance where you needed to be close to your partner, while he could drive an artic truck through my frame.

The frame! Improving my frame became the bane of my life. My posture was something I'd never been concerned about until now.

That was the first night of voting, and my backside was trending on social media: the pants were so tight it looked like they were painted onto me. In hindsight I should have reduced the squatting in the gym as the pants situation was painful!

It was the first night someone would be sent home, which was not easy as we had all put so much time into it and really didn't want to see someone go.

Hughie Maughan was eliminated that week, which was unfortunate as he was the character who made people laugh. We had great banter one day when he said he'd been looking at the bookies' odds and that they fancied I'd be gone home before him. As we were chatting, a few more entered the conversation: 'Sure what counties will vote for you, Aidan? Cork? No. Dublin? No.' The net was getting tighter but all I could do was laugh it off. In the back of my mind one of the reasons for taking part in *Dancing with the Stars* was so that people would get to see Aidan O'Mahony the person and not the footballer. I went into the show as myself and I didn't alter any part of that self.

After that, the pressure was off because I wasn't the first one eliminated, but I remember early on Lorraine Barry saying I needed to be putting in more time if I wanted to do well. Which is like everything you do in life: the more time you put in, the better you become. I think I had too much going on in my life compared to the other contestants and I wasn't based in Dublin.

I could see Lorraine's point, but as I've said, I was working my day job, building a house, Denise was pregnant, I was studying for a degree in strength and conditioning and keeping my fitness up by going to the gym daily. But I had learned from the path I'd taken in previous years that I would just put my head down, work hard, back myself and find a way to multi-task. Denise was supportive and positive as always and remained her usual independent self while I was on the show. She spent most weekends in Dublin with friends and family to attend the Sunday night show.

I was working Monday to Wednesday, heading to Dublin Thursday morning, a couple of 12-hour days and then rehearsals all day Saturday and the show Sunday.

Every minute of my life was scheduled, but looking back I wouldn't change it one bit as it was really exciting and unpredictable. The show could end any week for me with an elimination.

18

A New Arrival

Dancing for Joy

My dancing ability was mid-table material in sporting terms as the weeks progressed. This was acceptable but it also meant I'd have to improve to make the top four. Or the semi-finals, as I thought of it. My muscle memory was gradually improving as was my emotional intelligence for feeling the music and the lyrics.

When we got to week six, contestants switched up dance partners and I got partnered with Karen Byrne. Dublin and Kerry would finally unite, but not as I'd imagined! The hours were not invested this particular week due to a number of reasons on both sides.

We got slated when it came to the performance itself, and rightly so. The judges said there needed to be smoothness and fluency, none of which were visible in our efforts.

I didn't want to be remembered for that week, so that Sunday in particular I really didn't want to be eliminated. In addition, I didn't want go out that night given my reaction to Brian Redmond's comments. He had said something along the lines of 'there was plenty of bounce but this had no relation to a samba'. I replied that that's like asking him to come across the white lines of Croke Park with me. I respected his valid judgement, and my response towards him reflected the negative week I'd had. In hindsight those comments and that poor performance were the knock-back I needed to rediscover my determination for the weeks that followed. Thankfully, I wasn't in the bottom three that Sunday night, or indeed any Sunday night before or after.

I remember on the drive home to Kerry reminding myself that I had a new dance routine the following week. I would be reunited with Valeria and I would come out fighting to redeem myself.

It was like having a bad game, taking the positives and working on the negatives: was I going to give away my jersey, was I going to allow that performance, lack of commitment and costume define me? The answer was 'no'. I had been down that road before. Game on.

Valeria and I fought back. It was like getting knocked out of the championship but coming back in through the qualifiers, or getting dropped and making it back onto the team through your own determination.

I said to myself, *If you're going to be knocked out of this competition, at least go down fighting.*

For the next weekend we prepared a waltz and it went very well. We knew we'd prepared a good one and on the night Brian Redmond even said, 'We've got Aidan O'Mahony back and he's looking good.' He even said my frame was very good, which was high praise.

Still, I knew we could do better. The next week we had the Charleston and I came up on the Wednesday to rehearse, which was a day early for me. Most contestants would have had three days' rehearsing done when I arrived to the party. I remember Denise and her sisters regularly asking me what my routine was like for the approaching week and up to the Thursday all I could tell them was the name of the dance as I usually wouldn't have done a step of it until then.

However, week eight was different: 12 hours a day Wednesday, Thursday and Friday, lifts and turns, lifts and turns – the routine was full to the brim with content. And we had an extra input from Aoibhín and Vitali. We were rehearsing in the same studios and looking at each other's dances, and they were very good to point out little things we could do to improve.

On the Saturday we had rehearsals in the studio and it was the first time I heard people say 'Wow!' about our routine when we came off the floor: we knew we'd gone to another level and I could feel this in the air, literally. I had the energy, fitness, determination, competitiveness and strength – and the skill came gradually.

Because of my preparation that week, because we'd put that work in, because I'd listened to the judges about improving my frame and putting in more rehearsals, I felt very confident.

On the Sunday night we started with our individual pieces and then got into the Charleston routine together – Valeria spent more time over my head than on the dance floor, or at least that's how my arms felt afterwards – and it flowed from start to finish.

The crowd were electric, there was a great atmosphere, and for the ending I ran to a piano only for Valeria to bump me off onto the floor.

As I picked myself up I saw everyone in the audience on their feet. A standing ovation on week eight was the encouragement I needed and it was a hugely enjoyable moment, to have come so far in a few weeks. Now I started thinking that I should have invested more time in my routines.

The judges were glowing about the dance, and Julian Benson said, 'In week one I said you were a dark horse to win the competition, and now you're beginning to prove me right.'

Brian Redmond added, 'I said we were waiting for

someone from the middle of the group to push to the top three, and Mr O'Mahony, you have arrived.'

We got a nine from Brian, Lorraine gave us a ten and Julian gave us a nine.

It was a special feeling because it showed how far I had come after the setback in week six. Sometimes in life setbacks can drive you to a whole new level and I started to tell myself that I could win this show. So many skills are transferable in life and this time I called upon the skills and abilities I had acquired during my sporting career.

All of the elements had fed into it – the routine Valeria created, the support and advice from Denise, taking on board the judges' comments – and it had all paid off.

That night was bittersweet in one respect, though. I'd taken leave from work to stay up and rehearse during the week, because the competition had just reached that level and I needed to do that to keep pace with the others.

It was similar to falling in with pre-season training – if you don't have anything done you'll suffer and fall off. Myself, Dayl, Des, Aoibhín and Denise McCormack were left in the hunt at this stage, and I knew I needed to put more work into it, but there was another big event approaching.

Back home, Denise was also coming closer to her due date, so Valeria and I planned 12 hours of rehearsals on the Monday and Tuesday to free me up for the arrival later that week. There was a lot of work involved because we were dancing the cha-cha, and there was another dance needed for the couples dance-off.

The others lightened the week for me – there was lots of banter; Dayl was preparing me for fatherhood as he was like my child who I looked after every day! He went out and bought so many blue clothes for the new arrival that I wondered if he knew something I didn't. No, he just presumed it was a boy, he told me. I had to break the news to him that I already knew it was going to be a girl! It made me emotional when he presented me with so many gifts. Expecting a child is always an emotional time, but that week I was also so tired from the rehearsals. I gave him a big hug and headed off to Kerry.

A new person coming into our lives was such an overwhelming feeling. I was full of the joys of life coming home knowing that we were heading for Cork University Hospital on Thursday morning.

Lucia came into our lives at 9 a.m. that day. Anyone who's been through the experience will know the feeling when your baby is handed to you for the first time: you know that life is changing right in front of you. There are emotions running high, with tears of happiness flowing. And in the middle of all this ... people are asking me how *Dancing with the Stars* is going. It was the furthest thing from my mind at that time.

I stayed in the hospital the whole day and I'd say I spent most of it being emotional. I didn't want to go home but Denise insisted, so that I could get some rest. I drove over the border from Cork to Kerry, down the long hill towards Glenflesk and the turn off to Kenmare on my left – when suddenly a huge deer ran out in front of the car. But for whatever reason, the deer decided to stop halfway across the road and in doing so let me see another day. I knew in that moment that the man above was looking down on me.

Back to the hospital the following day; our loved ones were visiting to see the new arrival. That afternoon I got a call from *Dancing with the Stars* asking if we'd had a boy or a girl, but they also had a job to do and a show to put on: was I going to be back in the studio on Saturday? They needed me there, they needed VT, they needed costume fittings and they needed the competitor onsite.

Saturday came around and I knew I was scheduled to be at rehearsals at 4.30 p.m. – the show must go on. My sister Linda was in the hospital at the same time, as was Moira, my sister in-law, and I was saying that maybe I wouldn't bother going back.

I had tears flowing at this point from the exhaustion, the emotion and the view of our beautiful little Lucia with the darkest hair; I had become a dad and nothing else seemed to matter. However, I was encouraged to finish what I started by the ladies in the room.

I was congratulated when I got to the studio, but most people had gone home because rehearsals had finished.

Then they showed me my costume. An electric pink pants and shirt.

I had to challenge it. 'I haven't made an issue about costumes all through the show,' I said to the ladies, 'but I just had a baby girl and I am meant to wear all pink because of this?' They agreed to change the pants.

Valeria and I did our rehearsals and it got better and better as we progressed. It brought home the importance of muscle memory to me. In football you know what you're bringing to a game and because you've done those moves for so long it's second nature. At that stage I'd been doing so much dancing that it was coming more and more naturally to me.

I was also in great form, obviously enough. I had so much to look forward to with Denise and Lucia, and the dancing was coming to an end as well – and no matter how enjoyable it was, it had also been stressful. Now I felt I was able to relax and enjoy even the rehearsals that bit more.

Those rehearsals went so well they were calling me 'Daddy Cool'. Nicky Byrne came in with a present of Dublin baby GAA gear for Lucia: the atmosphere was great. There were pink balloons in every corner and everyone was so thoughtful with their well-wishes. The night finished with a live performance by Lyra of 'Emerald' which was a memorable moment and song from the whole *DWTS* experience.

The only downside was the departure of Des Cahill that evening.

We'd fallen into a routine on some Sunday nights where Dayl, myself and Des would go to Des's local after the live show. Des is such a genuine guy and it was a real blow when he was sent home because we'd become very close, but on the other hand it was week nine. The end was in sight, with just two shows left.

The playing field changed when Valeria agreed to come down to Kerry the following week to rehearse with me in Killarney. I rang the INEC and the O'Donoghues, the owners of the venue, were more than helpful, giving us the use of both the ballroom in the INEC and The Brehon. I would also make a bit of time to show Valeria the beauty of Killarney.

It all meant I was able to leave Dublin the following morning after the live show to collect Lucia and Denise in Cork and bring them home. That's the kind of moment you never forget, the first time you all head home as a family: an amazing feeling, and one that put everything in perspective.

When Valeria came down we worked hard on two full dances – the Viennese waltz and the jive. Our waltz was very good but I struggled with the jive.

When we headed back to Dublin it was St Patrick's Day. We all rehearsed that morning and I told Dayl that Dr Crokes were playing in the All-Ireland club final in

Croke Park and I was heading there to see them if he was interested.

We ended up going to the game and afterwards somewhere for a drink to wet the baby's head. Just to unwind.

Luckily our rehearsal slots weren't until the following afternoon, which gave us a mini rest the next morning. I was as much hungover from the emotion of the previous few days as from the beverages. That rehearsal was probably the worst: I was missing steps as we worked through it, which didn't make Valeria too happy.

But thankfully it started to come together after a couple of hours. The moves came back to me and I improved as the day progressed. That evening before going to bed I focused: I said I'd go out and give it everything in the show. I was very much aware that the other contestants left in the competition were outstanding performers, but as long as I did my best on the show, I'd be happy with that.

The dances went well on the night. The jive went fine but the Viennese waltz was excellent, I knew that. I told myself I'd done well to get to the semi-final stage. Though some people might have thought I had the GAA vote locked up, in my mind I was thinking, *Well, they won't be voting for me in Cork, or in Dublin, or in Tyrone ...*

I'd given it everything and enjoyed the experience. It

really just happened organically that people voted to keep me in and I was extremely grateful for the support.

If I was eliminated that week it wouldn't be so bad as I would be heading back to Kerry – back to Denise and Lucia. If that was the worst-case scenario I was certainly more than happy with it.

When the votes came in Valeria and I were the first through. She gave me a fist bump and said, 'That's your vote.'

I was half-embarrassed – the cameras caught my expression. Deep down I'd thought my time was up. I'd come from zero and improved every week, but I certainly didn't feel I was a better dancer than the other three, and I'd never claim to be. The crew on the set labelled me a 'flower', one that grew every week.

At the same time, people were very supportive of me and my place in the competition, and I was very much grateful for that. I had messages pointing out how far I'd come and highlighting that the show was about people improving and not entering with a high standard from week one. On consideration I accepted that and felt reassured about my position.

Dayl was sent home that evening, and he was emotional about it. He'd put a huge amount of work into it and my heart went out to him. It really made me sad to see him so upset. As I sat into the car that evening I felt I owed it to him to give the final my very best shot.

We had three intense dances to work on for that last week, but there was a bit of build-up ahead of the final. There was some filming in the garda station in Tralee, with a few of the lads showing off their dance moves – and of course all my colleagues had the opportunity to get the slagging in.

Valeria came to Tralee to rehearse in the School of Music, and she said we'd start with our show dance. Lift after lift after lift, and then a twist on that: I had to slip her up around the back of my neck, put my hands behind my back and then throw her from behind my neck to grab her in front. There wasn't a nanosecond to get distracted with those extreme lifts. The attention to detail had to be 100 per cent, otherwise the consequences would be disastrous. Valeria really trusted me with her life in relation to some of the lifts we executed for the final show.

Valeria stayed in the Brehon hotel while we rehearsed in Kerry. I remember her repeating how friendly and welcoming the people of Kerry were – she even mentioned it on live TV. Some of the VT that week was captured on a jaunting car around the beautiful lakes of Killarney. There was so much Kerry scenery in the four-minute VT, and seeing that in the live studio gave me huge pride. Valeria's opinion of the Kerry people she met was spot on: genuine, friendly, warm, helpful and extremely funny.

We put in a huge amount of work that week so that we'd be able to say afterwards that we'd left everything on the dance floor. Every lift that could possibly be done was done. It was just like an All-Ireland final, when you can say that morning, 'I've the work done. I'm ready.'

Back to Dublin on the Saturday for rehearsals. The American Smooth, the salsa – they went well, and then we finished with the show dance (to Bonnie Tyler's 'Holding Out for a Hero'). I was a little nervous, but ready. I can remember clearly thinking that the following morning it would all be over, and the experience would be just another chapter in my life. I couldn't wait to get back to my reality and my bubble. There were going to be no regrets, which was a major positive.

On the Sunday, Aoibhín Garrihy and Denise McCormack were fantastic. We were up first to perform on the night; it went well and we got a good score and a standing ovation. But then we were backstage to change immediately, so the whole experience really flew by.

My family and friends were there to support me and that motivated me even more to give it everything. Initially Denise wasn't going to attend the live show as Lucia was only two weeks, but the night before, she called me and told me she had changed her mind. 'If you win I will definitely regret it if I'm not there to hug you,' she said.

She was there and looked absolutely stunning as always despite being a little sleep-deprived. She'd been flying the plane alone since Lucia was born and had spent most of the third trimester without me. She was – and is – my positive rock.

Everyone there for me on the night was really rooting for me and that was driving me on. I was never as thankful for my fitness during the entire show, but especially on the final night. The fact that I was coming off years of training with Kerry and intensive gym programmes definitely stood to me in those weeks, because dancing 10 hours a day, doing lifts after lifts, takes it out of you. I was a stone and a half lighter in the last week than I was at the start because of all those rehearsals.

When the final dance routine finished, I put a fist in the air. It was over. Finally. I could get back to the life that I knew and loved. The relief was massive after nearly three months of travel, rehearsing, VTs, live shows, after-shows, interviews and overall intense concentration.

It was all in the lap of the gods when I turned to the judges: they gave us three tens and the positivity in their feedback was just fantastic. They reviewed how far I'd come over the three months; it gave me so much confidence.

Amanda Byram announced that the result was coming in, and myself and Valeria, Vitali and Aoibhín, and Denise and her dance partner Ryan all had to stand in the centre of the dance floor for the formal announcement, with the glitter ball in our sight.

Eleven of us had started and most of us didn't know each other but we'd built a very strong bond throughout our time there.

The silence was deafening as everyone waited for the result, my heart was beating quicker by the second … the shouts from the crowd, the tension and waiting was just unbelievable. When my name was called out as the winner I sank to my knees. It was like hearing the final whistle in a game, when the sound sends emotion flooding through you. For me it was probably the culmination of everything that had happened in the previous few weeks.

As I said that evening, it hadn't been about winning for me so much as doing something I never expected or thought I'd do. Proving to myself that I could do something totally new and different and succeed at it.

That's how I look at it in retrospect, as one of the biggest chances I ever took in my life. That might sound strange, but as an introvert it was a real step outside my comfort zone. It was definitely a chance I was glad I took.

It was also a great distraction for my mom, particularly after Dad's passing. The void after inter-county football was nothing compared to the void in her life when her best friend of 50 years had gone.

We met up with family and friends backstage and had a bit of a celebration. I'd organised a visit to Hugh Hourican in The Boar's Head after the show no matter what was planned for the night, and my family all went down there before we headed up to Café en Seine for the wrap party.

The morning after the show I headed in to Dublin city to do some interviews, and I ended up meeting nearly everyone all over again. I recall going in to Ryan Tubridy's show, which was held in the Shelbourne hotel. I said to him it was about the challenge and engaging with that, which was a big lesson I took out of the whole experience.

It's not a matter of what other people are doing, what journey they're on, so much as your own journey and what you make of that. The comparisons between sport and dancing didn't all stack up.

From day one I could see that dancing, the art, was everything to the pro dancer, and that I'd have to respect and comprehend that to have any hope of doing well. The instructors wanted to tell a story to the audience every week through the routines, which was something I had to take on board. My acting skills were non-existent but I gave it my best shot for the most part.

The dynamic in sport is that you're with 15 or 30 or more players trying to bring joy to your county or your club through victory. With dancing it was about sharing a story with the people watching.

On the other hand, the parallels between coaching in the two different fields were a lot stronger. I could see that even if someone had no background at all in a discipline, putting the time and effort into that person would make all the difference in improving their performance.

People often ask me now if I kept up the dancing. I didn't. I often repeat the moves around my kitchen, messing with my wife and kids. I often have banter with Denise, telling her that I was the best dancer in Ireland in 2017. I have attended a few weddings since then and around half eleven at night people start asking me to show them how to salsa or jive. Telling them there's a world of difference between rehearsing non-stop for three days, on the one hand, and a skip at a wedding, on the other, doesn't usually convince them that my moves aren't what they were on TV.

I wasn't back home too long after the show when Rathmore got in touch about the county championship. That was the reality check I needed.

The irony is that I was in fantastic shape after the dancing, and my feet were never as quick. I think if I'd been dancing in parallel with my football career there'd have been a huge dividend on the football field.

It's a great memory, particularly as it was a family show and a lot of people watched it with their loved ones.

Sometimes Lucia and Lilah, who was born in 2019, will say they want to watch Daddy dancing, and I put it up on YouTube for them. I know well that in a couple of years they might instead be covering their eyes in embarrassment.

It was an experience that contained a lot of lessons for me: about trying something new, about overcoming setbacks, about convincing yourself to persevere and to always be yourself even if there are cameras wanting otherwise.

Winning the competition was never really the point. That was the major bonus, but not as big a bonus as I got the morning after, back home. I was lying on the sofa, baby Lucia in the middle, Denise on the other side of her.

'No dancing rehearsals or lifts this week,' I said. 'Life is good.'

Retiring from inter-county football might have left a void, but this new chapter was the perfect antidote to that.

I learned about moving beyond my comfort zone, about taking on a new challenge, about recognising the artistry and professionalism in others. My takeaway was: rather than simply listing off all the reasons not to do something, try to see the benefits of a completely different set of challenges.

As a result, I think people saw a different side of me too.

19

Starting Out in Business

Towards the end of my playing career I was starting to look for the next step or chapter in my life. I loved the whole fitness side of things and wanted to dive deeper into it. I met with Dave Moriarty, a garda and strength and conditioning lecturer with Setanta College, and in 2016 during the national league I enrolled with Setanta, an internationally renowned centre of excellence for strength and conditioning and athletic development, and after a further conversation with Kevin Smith, student officer, I enrolled for a BSc degree in strength and conditioning.

It was great to get a focus beyond football; I'd always been interested in knowing the precise reasoning behind all the work we had been doing in preparation for match days and the course gave me just that. It spurred me on to push myself more, to push the boundaries and to start looking at the next challenge.

One idea I had always toyed with from a young age was owning my own business.

Combining the challenge of starting something new with putting that into a business context is where my cousin Michael O'Donoghue came in.

It was an idea that we had often bounced around, and in conversation Michael would ask me, 'Why don't you share your insight into your training?'

That idea got transformed into a five-year plan, and Michael sums up the journey perfectly on a recent podcast about the early days of the business.

We'd messaged back and forth for a couple of months about moving this idea forward, but it was April 2016 AOM Fitness really got moving. We had planned to meet the Tuesday after the 2016 league final between Kerry and Dublin. The next five days tells me everything you need to know about Aidan.

The Friday before we had planned to meet I had issued a 30-page document outlining how we were going to launch, the targets we were going to hit, a plan going forward, documented step by step, everything from the colour of the logo to the layout of the website to the format of the social media page; everything was mapped out to give us a starting point with basically a strategic plan for the first five years from set-up to fully functional.

It was all going well: Aidan liked the document; he had ideas on areas we could improve, notes done, ready to run through and get cracking on the Tuesday.

Then the Sunday before, 46 minutes into the league final – red card. Aidan gets a straight red, Kerry lose and the straight red means he misses the first game of the Munster championship.

Tuesday, I'm sitting in a coffee shop in Killarney, Aidan's en route, I'm thinking, How am I going to play this one, what interest will he have in this after what just happened on Sunday?

Instead Aidan bounces up the stairs; there's more a look of a man on a mission than a sulk. There isn't a mention of what's happened, and instead he outlines how he must be into Kerry training early for 'prehab work'.

We meet four hours before Kerry team training. Aidan's into training two hours later (two hours before training starts). Now we share heart-rate monitors so we can see each other's sessions – for an hour and a half, this 'prehab session' before his team training, as I expected, had heart-rate outputs of those similar to high-intensity work rather than the so-called 'prehab work' he mentioned.

Three days later we meet again to start moving the AOM Fitness idea forward. This document took me the bones of a year to put together, it had everything from trends on social media, which e-commerce system to implement on the website, costings to set up and run, how and when we were going to launch. I was full of confidence, ready to run through.

On the previous Tuesday Aidan's action was to go away and pull out any training content we could put together from what training he had done.

It's not an exaggeration when I say his kitchen had turned into a library; there were boxes upon boxes, labelled by year, broken down into off-season, pre-season and on-season, segregated into each month.

All results, amount lifted, times run, distance covered, you name it, all noted. And at the end a personal summary on the session: what went well, what didn't, what needed improvement. This went on from 2003 up until the present day.

Basically, my 30-page document got lost in among a 14-year mountain of day-by-day training journals.

Two days in, I finally understand what people mean about Aidan when they say 'no stone unturned', 'try to stop him'.

I pride myself on my preparation and my years of journalling and note-taking, and combining that with my further studies, and with all that starting to align with Michael's plan, it was a no-brainer.

Phase 1 was to launch a blog-style website, just tabling my thoughts on training, sample sessions and generally just putting pen to paper on what worked or didn't work for me. We spent the summer of 2017 doing just that, both of us tasked to write down as much content as possible; then winter 2017 was all about filming.

We both work full time. I'm a garda and Michael's a commercial manager, and we live in different countries. Between balancing the above and other commitments, our window of opportunity is narrow when we do get a chance to get together.

When we first started filming content, it was a solid three to four days' work. Michael would fly into Kerry airport on a Friday night, I would collect him and we would head straight to the first filming location – a floodlit pitch or a gym.

We've had a lot of help along the way, which we're very grateful for – Michael's school friend Sean Howley (a videographer) was brought in to help with the filming and editing and I wouldn't even begin to try and work out the hours he put in for us.

Joe O'Connor was another big help: he's an established strength and conditioning coach with notable success with Clare, Limerick and Kerry GAA teams. He's a close friend of mine, a gym owner in Tralee who without hesitation would give me the keys to his gym, Nisus Fitness, to film content.

A lot of our early content was filmed in there, but being a successful gym we could only film out of hours. It would often entail starting filming after closing at 9 p.m. and working right through into the early hours. We often did this on back-to-back nights as well.

Those early days were tough, but the drive and excitement from all involved energised us through any late night or long weekend. The lessons I'd learned from previous experiences about dedicating myself to a task and applying myself to achieve came in very useful, as always – even though I was applying them to a completely different area of my life – and I'm always happy to learn something new as well. Getting to that final point was the driver in the early days, but reflecting back now, it also makes us proud of what we have built.

After a long summer and winter, our content was all filmed, edited and up on the temporary site, so the final part was to put together a launch video to push out on the social media pages to introduce our site to all.

It's funny how things work out: we had our launch video almost finished, with the sticking point being the last clip to close it. We needed a big finish and the idea was to show a 'reaching the summit' clip.

We had searched everywhere and just couldn't find the right location. While we were casting around to see what might work I got a call inviting me to judge a *Strictly Come Dancing* event in Bantry.

A fine, cold January evening on the old Kenmare road to Bantry and my sat nav went wrong: somewhere around Kilgarvan I took a turn and went off up a mountain.

I was getting worried when I started passing patches of snow, but the road eventually came to a peak, with a 200-foot sheer drop.

I got out to have a look and to record a video of the scene to show Michael; a car passed me and I'd say I made a fine sight, decked out in a suit, the snow falling as I was filming the cliff on my phone. The driver slowed down just to make sure he wasn't seeing things, I'd say.

The location was exactly what we needed, the scenery perfect, and far out in the distance you could even get a glimpse of my dad's farm. Coincidence?

On 23 April 2018 we launched the website on 2FM. I remember driving to Dublin and, typical of me, I was so determined not to get caught on the M50 that I was in the RTÉ car park at a quarter to nine that morning. The launch was half ten. You can't be too careful.

Nicky Byrne and Jenny Greene had me on and they were very good, because I hadn't slept a wink the night before.

The build-up to the launch had been a two-year assignment, so there was no sleep the night before – instead time was spent checking every detail on the site, from the font size on the blog post to the loading time of each workout video.

Checking lasted right up until I was walking into the studio. I remember being on the phone to Michael while sitting in the RTÉ car park, just doing test launches over and over.

AOM Fitness was fully funded by both of us and no corner was cut. We'd both have a keen eye for the little details, so everything had to be perfect.

On that opening week we averaged 16,000 people on the site at any one time.

We released a launch video on our social media platforms to coincide with the website launch, which gained combined views of over a million in the first week.

The first year we played catch-up – the site was getting visited from all over the world – with direct messages. Just keeping up with them was a challenge in itself, but that's something we take pride in, being that point of contact.

Likewise the invitation to attend events, to partner with companies and brands, was another challenge in terms of picking the right fit for us, all taking time to give the necessary review before jumping in.

A big milestone for us was getting invited into Google HQ; there was a huge sense of excitement, but also pride in the recognition the site was getting on Google's radar. It was a full-day visit, reviewing where we were as a business and where we were headed. A real eye-opener, with huge knowledge gained.

One key action on the back of the visit was the encouragement to connect with our audience more, so we decided to start a weekly question and answer slot on our Instagram page, where every Thursday our followers can ask a question on any subject. The questions are private, with the answers shared for others to view.

If I'm honest, I was hesitant at first, mindful of the questions that would come and also the possible lack of them.

Each week we now get on average 6,000 people engaging in the Q&As, with questions covering all aspects of training, recovery, nutrition and my career.

The one subject area that I wasn't expecting was in relation to mental health. It's staggering, but it's one we've tracked and targeted as an area to help, with 35 per cent of the weekly questions relating to mental health.

Since the start of the Covid pandemic we have noticed a large increase in the number of questions on this topic. There is no doubt that people of all ages, but particularly younger people, have experienced mental health issues due to lockdowns, lack of social engagement and many of the other restrictions that were imposed. At AOM Fitness we have done our best to give people encouragement during this difficult time, and hopefully as life returns to normal, mental health for those impacted will continue to improve.

The originators of this 35 per cent are all between the ages of 18 and 24. There are some questions where I can't share the answers with the audience, so instead I get in contact with the person directly.

I feel I can relate to some of these, that I'd been that person at different times in my career. I feel a responsibility to make myself available and I haven't missed a Thursday night yet. One of the founding principles of AOM Fitness was to be that point of contact, and that 35 per cent enforces that responsibility.

Looking back to when I started off in adult football 20-odd years ago, as a shy youngster in Rathmore I'd have found it a huge help to touch base with someone who'd been through the mill – to be able to send them a question on a Thursday night.

Advice on my training would have been one of the first questions asked. We noticed this need and, in line with our five-year plan, we launched our first downloadable training programme.

The programme 'Muscle & Movement' was released in 2019: a 39-page document, covering six weeks of an individual off-season training programme. It was picked up worldwide, with participants accessing the programme from every continent.

The locations and number of downloads is one thing, but nothing fills you with pride as much as seeing the results and hearing of the improvements being made. Both of us put a lot of time and money into getting AOM Fitness off the ground. Its original intention was to share my training insights/workouts, which we thought might be of interest to a local – or, best-case scenario, Irish – audience, but what was to follow was not expected in terms of scale and reach, as we've now worked with the likes of Google, Sport Ireland, and we've also featured with numerous government incentives and have secured partnerships with Ireland's leading sports nutrition and equipment suppliers.

We have found ourselves branching into other sports, meeting with the likes of FIFA's strongest man, Adebayo Akinfenwa, to put plans in place for the year ahead.

With all the success, though, what drives us on is that one comment or direct message from someone who has made progress thanks to a piece of content or programme that we have put out. That's what makes it all worthwhile.

> The business has grown and grown, and the lesson weaves other experiences together – I learned to back myself, in football and in *Dancing with the Stars*, and I relied on the self-belief I built through all the setbacks in a long career, on the field of play and in civilian life. I also learned that everyone makes mistakes – some things work out and some things don't – but I would always do my best at whatever I put my mind to, and I would try not to think about other people's expectations or judgements.

My past experiences have combined to build the confidence I have in myself to deal with people in the Q&A sessions – the interaction is open and helpful, and I'm a lot more open myself, even if it was a fair journey for me to reach this point.

20

A New Set of Challenges

Dipping My Toe in the Water

In September 2019 I went on the Portuguese camino as an ambassador for CRY (Cardiac Risk in the Young), which was a journey of reflection, appreciation and planning. Some of the things I thought about while on the pilgrimage were overcoming my fear of swimming, writing this book and becoming more mindful and appreciative of life.

The camino was a unique experience and one I will never forget because of the people I met along the way. I undertook this journey with 22 others, including my wife Denise. I formed a close bond with everyone I walked with and maintain regular contact with them to this day. Our walk was part of the Portuguese Coastal Way, and each pilgrim had their own spiritual and reflective reasons for going on the trip. I had the opportunity to hear so many stories, most of which were heart-breaking. There were many stops along the way to scatter ashes of loved ones and to tell another story of life's struggles.

Leaving the camino, I wrote down a number of challenges I wanted to face when I got home, and learning to swim and overcoming my fear of deep water was top of the list. I no longer wanted to procrastinate on facing some of my lifelong fears.

I have two kids and I didn't want to be left on the beach or at the side of the pool if they were swimming and happened to seek my help and I couldn't swim.

One afternoon in the garda station a pal and colleague of mine, John Gilmartin, suggested that due to my competitive streak I should think about taking up triathlons. I told him I'd really like to, but that while I could run and cycle with determination, I wasn't sure how I would do with the swimming as I was just starting out with that. I started a course in Olympic lifting with UKSCA, which included being assessed in competent lifting. My first day trying out the Olympic lifts didn't go as planned, as it highlighted my poor mobility and flexibility. I had always heard that swimming was excellent for mobility and so there were many reasons for me now to give swimming a go.

I was encouraged to get a good wetsuit and head out into the open water in Fenit. I got a few names to make contact with to see if they would take me on board and coach me.

Within half an hour I left the garda station and walked up to Waterworld to purchase what I needed.

I was asked one question when I entered: Are you a confident swimmer? I explained that I'd had a few lessons in the pool and had practised for a few weeks in the garda college. I told them I'd need something that would give me all the help in the world, and with that I got my first Orca wetsuit. I jumped on social media and contacted Kevin Williams, a swimming coach, and we got started.

The first drive out to Fenit was daunting. As I passed The Spa, the sun was shimmering across the water all the way to Derrymore beach, and my heart was racing with fear and anxiety. I used to have nightmares about the sea and not being able to survive if I were ever to get into danger.

The wetsuit was hanging in the back of the car, swaying back and over as I turned each bend, as though it was trying to tell me something. I landed at Fenit beach and could see the lighthouse in the distance: the water was calm and the breeze was just perfect. That first sight will always stick with me.

I met Kevin Williams: first impressions last and he really put me at ease. I'm not sure what his first impressions were of me, though, as he saw me put on my little white gloves to put on the wetsuit without scratching and try to pour myself into my new wetsuit, a challenge before I'd even entered the water.

I found I really enjoyed the lessons. The scenery alone in Fenit would lift anyone's mood. We were making good progress: in four feet of water I was as confident a swimmer as you could find.

I bought a Garmin watch and could begin to see myself in the triathlon itself, coming out of the sea and getting on my bike ... This goal provided motivation to keep going.

One morning Kevin said, 'You're covering 50, 60 metres – let's see if you can do 100 metres this morning.'

I did about 130 metres, and Kevin was very impressed: 'That's amazing, but what was different about this morning compared to other mornings?'

'That's easy,' I said. 'This was the first morning I could look down through the water and see the crabs on the sea floor. I was afraid to look down and there was no way I was putting a foot down on them.'

He asked if I had a fear of them, and I said straight out that I had a fear of everything in the water.

'But the crabs can't do anything to you,' he said.

'I know, but every night before I go swimming that fear pops into my head.'

And that fear popped into my head again a few days later, when Kevin pointed towards a buoy and said, 'We'll swim out to that now.'

I froze. It was only about 50 metres out but there was no way I was getting out there. 'I can't,' I said.

'Why not?'

'Because my feet need to be touching the ground.'

He tested me, saying the wetsuit would keep me up, but there was no persuading me: I was comfortable in four feet of water where I could always put my feet on the ground and I knew that heading to that first buoy meant I would be out of my comfort zone.

'Okay,' he said. 'We'll wait until next week.'

The next session I landed on to the beach with my heart pumping in my chest. And like any good coach, instead of asking me to go as far as the buoy, he just said, 'I'm going to grab my goggles and we're going to swim out there.'

I wasn't panicking as we swam out; Kevin was swimming beside me and he was telling me not to fight the water, and I made it as far as the first buoy.

The sense of satisfaction, of doing something new, was huge. I honestly felt like I had achieved the impossible, looking back at the beach and thinking I had conquered one of my greatest fears. Then the sense of reality kicked in, because I knew I'd have to swim back in, but it was still a milestone. That feeling alone was worth the fear and anxiety in the lead-up.

When we came out of the water we embraced, and I told him he'd never know what that had done for my confidence. Driving home that day from the beach, it was like I'd achieved something real.

John Gilmartin, who'd put me onto the open-water swimming in the first place, was a huge help to me as well. We started to go swimming out by the diving boards off Fenit pier in the evenings and that built up my confidence.

In my next session after my first swim out to the buoy, I made it out as far as the second buoy and further. It was like any other goal-setting I had done in my life.

The swimming draws on a lot of my past experiences: how to rely on myself and the benefits of moving out of my comfort zone. I really had a fear of deep water growing up, but since we had the girls, I was determined to get to grips with swimming so I could be confident with them in the water as they got older, whether on holidays abroad or on a trip to the beach in Ireland. And seeing my progress during those sessions made me realise that just because something didn't come easily to me was not a reason to shy away from trying it and setting myself a goal. I just needed to be realistic about what those goals were.

I'd been on garda duty at the Tralee triathlon for a few years and as the contestants passed me by I'd always said to myself, *I'd love to be part of this.* I'd watched the Tralee Tri Club training and I knew it was something I wanted to do; they are a very close-knit group and very committed and driven.

I signed up for the triathlon without hesitation. But then Covid came along, Fenit was closed for a few weeks, and so I wasn't ready to compete. I had to put it on hold.

That just meant another challenge down the line. From my first day learning how to swim I had put content up on the AOM Fitness social media pages, just to show people how difficult I was finding it. Rather than trying to paint a false picture of everything being achievable, I wanted people to see how hard it was for me to learn a new skill, and to encourage them to try something similar.

People responded too. The day I froze and couldn't get out to the buoy, I got a lot of messages supporting me. Something didn't happen for me but there were helping hands extended by people who could sympathise.

I've also taken on other challenges since stepping away from the inter-county scene. Before I started playing football at a high level I really enjoyed playing soccer, and in 2018 I fell in with Killarney Athletic at centre-back. I loved it – training once a week, on a Friday, and then a match on Sunday, so it wasn't nearly as time-consuming as football. I got a massive buzz out of it.

The same year, my sergeant in Tralee, Tim O'Keeffe, and another garda colleague, Kevin Walsh (two guys with a fierce competitive edge) suggested one day that we go for a run on the road after work. I didn't realise we would run 10 kilometres, and when I came back I had pains in my shins and knees and everywhere else. I started to tell myself that road-running couldn't be good for me: I had spent a lifetime running on a pitch and the odd blow-out on the beach.

Tim advised me to get a good pair of trainers, and when I did they made a dramatic difference. We started running 10K three times a week and we ran an official half-marathon in July 2018 – the Killarney half-marathon from Moll's Gap, my first.

It was a fantastic experience. Having been in the football bubble for so long I didn't realise the number of events there are for people across all sports and at all levels, but the buzz up in Moll's Gap around half six in the morning was unbelievable; the rain was pelting down and I loved every minute of knowing what lay ahead, and then at the finishing line down in the Gleneagle hotel … We ran it in about 1:39 and it was great to finish in that timeframe. We were more than happy with that.'

I got such a kick out of it that we both signed up for the Dingle half-marathon – if any runner in Ireland ever wants scenery, this is the one – and we had a plan to improve our time. We'd stay with the 1:40 pacemaker from the beginning and break away before the finish.

There was a huge crowd and myself and Tim were dipping in and out from groups. We were late for the run and found ourselves at the back of the group, showing our lack of experience – we decided we needed to go full tilt once we crossed the starting line and tried to pass people at every avenue we could, but every time you cross over and back on the road you're burning up more energy, and when we got to 10 or 11 kilometres we were out on our feet.

Going up Slea Head I was struggling a little, my mind was asking me a lot of tough questions, the road seemed to be never-ending: would I give up, could I even make it?

As I crawled up the hills some fella cruised past me saying, 'Did you ever think you'd be going up Slea Head like this?'

All I could respond with was: 'If I don't see it again for a long time I'll be a happy man.'

I was surprised at the amount of conversation there is during a half-marathon.

Towards the end, one of the runners said, 'Four hundred metres to the end, lads,' but another guy piped up behind me, 'That's a kilometre, don't be making a burst at this stage.' A few hundred metres further up we passed Mr Four Hundred Metres sitting in the ditch. In every sport you need to take the right advice!

We finished the run and sat into the bus to take us back to the starting point, and I was looking in awe at the athletes doing the full marathon as they went past.

We'd got there in 1:36, which was good enough for me given the number of climbs involved. It was even better when we learned later that there hadn't been a 1:40 pacemaker in the race at all. We had run our legs off trying to catch him from the start, and the crowd in the bus got some laugh out of the two of us, pale as ghosts from exhaustion.

It was a revelation to me, the camaraderie and support among the runners – people coming up and asking how I'd found it. You think you'll never replicate the buzz of All-Ireland final day or winning *Dancing with the Stars*, but there are hundreds of people supporting, chatting, hugging and encouraging each other at an event like that.

There are elite athletes who are going flat to the mat from start to finish, but there's room for plenty of other people as well, and everyone doing what they can.

I would never have seen myself taking on something like that, but now my attitude is different. I see events like triathlons or half-marathons as open-door invitations.

Denise loves running as well, and it's a good example for the kids, to see their parents active and trying different sports rather than being tied to one and categorised: 'Your dad was a footballer so you'll play football.'

If they want to play football, that's fine, but if they want to take up running, or dancing, or anything else, that's fine too.

Trying different sports and disciplines is the important thing, not whether you fail or succeed.

I haven't done a triathlon yet, but plan on rectifying that very soon … and that's part of the broader picture.

And now there is the prospect of swimming with Denise and the kids – at a beach in Kerry or a swimming-pool on holidays.

One lesson for me is that no matter how good you think you are at a particular activity, there'll always be another activity, such as swimming for me, that will present a challenge. But putting the effort in allowed me to conquer another fear, and helped in practical ways as well.

Sometimes in life we can see challenges and obstacles as presenting a situation with no way out – I know I used to – but there is always a way out. It's about searching in your soul, but you also need to allow those closest to you to give you a helping hand. And for that to happen, you need to open up to them and drop that barrier you have put up. I've done so many school talks, team talks, business talks where you're introduced with a summary of what you have achieved and won in your career and where you are now, which I believe gets a lot of young people thinking 'I will never get to the level he did'. That was a big reason for me to write this book. You don't need to be the best. And obstacles and hurdles are part of life: it's all about getting over them or through them. It's about backing your self, surrounding yourself with positive people and always asking for help when needed.

I'm not sure what's going to come next in my life or what the next challenge will be. All I know is that

I've learned to stop worrying about other people's expectations and opinions. I know too that I have my family and loved ones by my side and that, right now, life is full of possibilities.

Acknowledgements

To all my family – I am grateful for your presence in my life and sharing the journey with me. Many thanks to my six siblings for supporting me through the challenges and celebrating the highs together.

To my wife Denise, daughters Lucia and Lilah, thank you for all the love, happiness and precious moments that you have brought to my life and I will cherish the memories forever and look forward to adding more chapters to the story.

To everyone who played a part in this book and its events, I am truly grateful.